From Family Literacy to Earth System Science

RESEARCH REPORT 1977–2018

DENNY TAYLOR

Denny Taylor's Research

on Making the Planet a Child Safe Zone

Contents.

Feature // **Integrating Knowledge**

24
Integrating Knowledge: First Response Initiatives in the Aftermath of Disaster

6
Urban and Rural Family Literacy Research

10
International Declaration of Family Literacy Principles.

12
Analysis of Political Campaign to Control How Children Learn to Read

14
Using Literacy to Create Caring Communities at Hofstra University

18
International Center for Everybody's Child

20
Fieldwork on Children and Armed Conflict

26
Fieldwork on Catastrophic Events: Hurricane Katrina

28
Using Literacy to Respond to Catastrophes

36
Human Activity and Atmospheric and Ecosystem Stressors

40
Teachers Respond to Hurricane Sandy and Sandy Hook Massacre

46
Garn Press: Supporting Writers of Conscience

52
Transdisciplinary Research Graphics

Introduction.

FAMILY LITERACY IS A GLOBAL CONCEPT
THAT CAN BE TRACED BACK TO DENNY TAYLOR'S
DOCTORAL RESEARCH

The concept of "family literacy" originated in the doctoral research of Denny Taylor. Recently colleagues and students have nominated her for several research awards in recognition of her lifetime commitment to transdisciplinary family literacy scholarship and fieldwork with families living in urban and rural poverty in the U.S., and in regions of armed conflict and catastrophic events around the world. This document was constructed to support one of the awards for which she has been nominated.

Every study Denny Taylor has undertaken in the past forty years is interconnected and reflects her deep commitment to culturally relevant research grounded in the everyday lives of families and communities. Her research encourages local contextualized changes that are historically and politically situated, and she has had a global impact in raising awareness of the systemic complexity of language, literacy and learning in diverse family and community settings throughout the world. Verification of the importance of the concept of family literacy is provided by the more than 7,000,000 Internet search results for "family literacy" and 5,640,000 for "family literacy nights", and of the importance of Denny Taylor's family literacy research by over 1,100 citations in academic publications to her scholarly work.

There are family literacy centers and coalitions across the United States, and many governments around the world have adopted the concept of family literacy. UNESCO uses family literacy as an organizing principle for the support of vulnerable populations and in 2012 published *A Handbook of Family Literacy*. There are family literacy programs in China, and among the countries that have family literacy programs for refugee women and their children are Somalia, Sudan, Iraq, Afghanistan, Iran, and The Democratic Republic of Congo. The remarkable fact is that there are now family literacy initiatives in every Member State of the United Nations.

Catherine Compton-Lilly, Rebecca Rogers, and Tisha Y. Lewis report that Denny Taylor is one of the most cited researchers in the field of family literacy, along with Shirley Brice Heath (MacArthur Genius Award) and Luis Moll (American Academy of Science). In 2012 in the *Reading Research Quarterly*, these researchers write:

> The four most cited researchers all conducted descriptive qualitative research projects that focused on culture, language, social class, and/or race. These studies included ... Denny Taylor's (1983; Taylor & Dorsey-Gaines, 1988) research with European American and African American Families. ... Postmodern stances are discernable in these descriptive studies in that they documented a limitless range of potential literacy practices and purposes (p. 42).

Compton-Lilly, Rogers, and Lewis provide a brief history of family literacy politics and programs stating, "Historically, U.S. policies have identified family literacy as a potential solution to economic and social disparities. During the 1980's, multiple family literacy programs were established through public and private efforts" (p. 34). These researchers also note, "Family literacy efforts have emerged around the world. Park (2008) studied the effects of children's home literacy on later reading achievement in 25 countries, including Singapore, Argentina, Colombia, and Iran, as well as European countries" (p. 34).

PHOTO: Denny Taylor began organizing family literacy nights in 1981. Family Literacy Nights are now ubiquitous in the U.S. and around the world. Here a graduate student and her children participate in a Family Literacy Night at Hofstra.

> Issues concerning equity and justice are embedded in our beliefs and understandings about literacy. Denny Taylor's research has been instrumental in placing family literacy at the center of such understandings

The Idea of "Family Literacy".

FAMILY LITERACY
YOUNG CHILDREN LEARNING TO READ AND WRITE
HEINEMANN (1983 & 1998)

Denny Taylor entered a transdisciplinary doctoral program with the sole intention of studying families and literacy, and the first paper she wrote in the first course she took with Hope Jensen Leichter in the fall semester of 1977 became the basis for the second chapter of her dissertation *Family Literacy: the Social Context of Young Children Learning to Read and Write*. Subsequently, every theoretical or field based paper she wrote during her doctoral studies focused on some aspect of families and literacy. The term "family literacy" emerged early in her studies, and she had many discussions with her mentor and doctoral chair Hervé Varenne about her interest in using family literacy as a central organizing principle in her dissertation. Varenne encouraged her to establish that "family literacy" was different from other sorts of literacies, and she embraced the challenge to demonstrate the existence of family literacy through disciplined and systematic observation of families using literacy in their everyday lives. She argued that it was possible to describe the phenomenon, but she resisted narrow definitions of the concept of family literacy arguing that a hard-edged definition would reduce the dynamic complexity of the idea.

Denny Taylor completed her dissertation research in the summer of 1980 and defended her dissertation in November of that year. However, because she had completed her doctorate in such a short period of time, her mentor and doctoral chair asked if she would defer until January 1981 and she agreed. In 1981 her dissertation was one of the ten outstanding dissertations recognized by the International Reading Association (now the International Literacy Association), and Heinemann published it with the title *Family Literacy: Young Children Learning to Read and Write* in 1983, with a second edition in 1988. It is now considered a classic in the field. In the foreword to the second addition Yetta M. Goodman writes:

> Issues concerning equity and justice are embedded in our beliefs and understandings about literacy. Denny Taylor's research has been instrumental in placing family literacy at the center of such understandings (p. vii).

On the completion of her doctorate, staying true to her Welsh coalmining roots Denny Taylor followed a different path than her peers. She accepted an honorary position offered to her by Charles Harrington as a Senior Research Fellow at the Institute of Urban and Minority Education at Teachers College, Columbia University. Thus she embarked on 20 years of fieldwork in urban and rural communities with families living in extreme poverty in the margins of American society. .

Longitudinal Fieldwork with Urban African American Families With Young Children Successfully Learning to Read and Write.

GROWING UP LITERATE
LEARNING FROM INNER-CITY FAMILIES
HEINEMANN (1988)

In January 1982 Denny Taylor began this intense ethnographic research phase of her life with four years of participation in the everyday lives of African American families with young children successfully learning to read and write, who were living in abandoned buildings and substandard housing in Newark, New Jersey. Catherine Dorsey-Gaines, the renowned African American scholar, encouraged Denny Taylor to undertake this study, and they were co-researchers on the project, which received the Elva Knight Award from the International Reading Association. In 1988 Heinemann published the book based on the study entitled *Growing Up Literate, Learning From Inner City Families*. In 1989 Denny Taylor and Catherine Dorsey-Gaines were the recipients of the Ninth Annual Mina P. Shaughnessy Prize awarded by the Modern Language Association of America for *Growing Up Literate*. The key ideas emerging from the research were:

- To be literate is a uniquely human experience, one that enables us to deal with ourselves and better understand one another. It is never a mechanical process that is solely dependent on skills that are taught;

- Race, gender, economic status and setting cannot be used as significant correlates of literacy;

- Literacy is not always liberating.

Longitudinal Fieldwork with Families of Appalachian Descent Living in Rural Poverty.

TOXIC LITERACIES
EXPOSING THE INJUSTICE OF BUREAUCRATIC TEXTS
HEINEMANN (1996)

This ethnographic work with African American urban families was followed by fieldwork in a rural town in New Hampshire, where Denny Taylor spent 12 years working with families of Appalachian descent living in rural poverty. Many of the adults she worked with were homeless and suffering from alcoholism and/or opioid and heroin addiction. An essential aspect of Denny Taylor's participation in the lives of these families was her advocacy for them when they tried to navigate the social welfare, healthcare, and criminal justice systems. Insights into the depth of her commitment to the families with whom she worked is indicated by her assuming the guardianship of a man who was homeless and a chronic alcoholic so he could receive the social welfare benefits otherwise denied to him. Participants in the project presented at national conferences with Denny Taylor, including an ethnography conference at the University of Pennsylvania. The research became the basis of the book *Toxic Literacies: Exposing the Injustice of Bureaucratic Texts*, (1996), which was nominated by Heinemann for a Pulitzer Prize and for the National Book Award. The cover description states:

> *Toxic Literacies* introduces us to Cindy, Sam, Laurie, Will, and Kathryn. Cindy is reinvented on paper and sent to prison, even though she has never stolen or hurt anybody. Forms are used to keep Sam homeless. Reports are written to justify why Laurie is crippled by radiation when she should have had surgery. Forms are used to exclude Will from his family. And the documents surrounding Kathryn's life eventually forced her to give up her baby.
>
> Through these individuals – people like so many we pass on the street every day – we experience how bureaucratic texts dictate lives. We see how people with power and privilege take control of language and use it for their personal advantage.

Fieldwork With Rural Families With Children Experiencing Difficulties At School Learning to Read and Write.

LEARNING DENIED
INAPPROPRIATE EDUCATIONAL DECISION MAKING
HEINEMANN (1990)

Concomitant with this fieldwork in a rural community, Denny Taylor also spent time with rural families with children experiencing difficulties at school learning to read and write. It was at this time that she undertook the landmark family literacy study of one child (Patrick) and his family that was published in a book entitled *Learning Denied: Inappropriate Educational Decision Making* (1990), which is still used in undergraduate and graduate literacy and special education courses both in the U.S. and abroad. In the foreword William L. Wansart writes:

> In *Learning Denied*, Denny Taylor tells the story of a family's clash with public school, special education bureaucracy. It is a personal story of Claudia and Pat as they attempted first to help their son Patrick in school and then, ultimately, to protect him from the school. It is also a cautionary tale of educational decision making gone wrong — a tale of reliance on a legalistic decision-making process that allows the participants to forget that there is a real child involved; a tale of a prevailing assessment paradigm that reduces learning to the scores on standardized tests; and the cumulative interpretive myth of "experts" who have rarely worked with, or every tried to teach, the child; where the focus is on what a child is unable to do rather than on what the child is capable of doing.

The Biographic Literacy Profiles Project: Fieldwork With Teachers and Children in Rural Public Schools.

TEACHING WITHOUT TESTING
ASSESSING THE COMPLEXITY OF CHILDREN'S LITERACY LEARNING
GARN PRESS (2017)

Denny Taylor's research and advocacy for Patrick and his family led to an invitation for her to work with public school teachers and children in rural schools in New Hampshire, which focused on the ethnographic documentation of children's observable literacy behaviors, with a special emphasis on children whose early literacy behaviors sometimes puzzle us. One hundred and twenty teachers and 1,200 children participated in what became known as the Biographic Literacy Profiles Project (BLiPP).

Teachers presented at national and international conferences with Denny Taylor, and the research received the 1990 National Council of Teachers of English Award (NCTE) for creating Six Centers of Excellence for Students at Risk. An account of the project was published in *From The Child's Point of View* (1993), and one chapter documenting the ethnographic observations of children writing has now been published by Garn Press as a separate book entitled *Teaching Without Testing: Assessing the Complexity of Children's Literacy Learning* (Edited by Bobbie Kabuto, 2017). In a memo to the teachers participating in the project dated September 16, 1991, Denny Taylor wrote:

> In the last couple of years, I think we have begun to understand that the Biographic Literacy Profiles Project is as much about ourselves as it is about children. It is about teachers developing personal theories, about teachers using their practical knowledge and theoretical expertise, and about teachers recognizing themselves, and being recognized by others, as professionals in their classrooms, schools and communities.

> When we observe children and write descriptions of their observable literacy behaviors we are creating critical sites of inquiry in our classrooms and in our schools. This is what BLiPP is all about. Learning to observe children and then learning to construct descriptions of their observable literacy behaviors encourages us to look at ourselves and our personal and shared ways of knowing. It is amazing stuff if you stop to think about it!

(Other studies that Denny Taylor undertook at this time included cultural-historical research on multigenerational patterns of conservation and change in a Welsh coal-mining village, and an ethnographic study of intergenerational participation in a village community theater production of the musical *Oliver*.)

The Development of An International Declaration of Family Literacy Principles.

MANY FAMILIES, MANY LITERACIES
AN INTERNATIONAL DECLARATION OF PRINCIPLES
HEINEMANN (1997)

A move to Arizona to teach masters and doctoral courses at the University of Arizona while the renowned scholars Ken and Yetta Goodman were on sabbatical afforded Denny Taylor with an opportunity to organize a working conference on family literacy. It was at this time that she invited scholars from around the world to spend a weekend in Tucson to develop a Declaration of Principles on Families and Literacy. With $5,000 from Heinemann to pay for a hotel conference center, Denny Taylor invited scholars from around the world to participate in the development of an International Declaration of Principles. All but one of the scholars who were invited accepted her invitation, travelling from across the United States, Canada, Mexico, the United Kingdom, and from as far away as South Africa and Australia. The major categories of the Declaration of Family Literacy Principles follow:

- Families have the right to define themselves;
- Families share the social, cultural, economic, and contexts of their everyday lives;
- Families are the primary literacy resource for their children;
- Racial and ethnic identity should not be used explicitly or implicitly to suggest that families live in households that lack social and intellectual resources;
- All languages have an equal potential to convey the full range of human thought and experience;
- A fundamental right of every family is to be literate in the language of their choice;
- Like all languages, literacy develops in response to everyday needs;
- Families continually develop and share their literacies – including marginalized and often unrecognized local literacies;
- Literacy is embedded in different ideologies, in different political perspectives and their consequences vary situationally;
- No single, narrow definition of family literacy can do justice to the richness and complexity of families and literacy;
- Educators should recognize the expertise of families and view all family members as knowledgeable, capable learners;
- At the core of any locally developed literacy program are the reciprocal practices that are established between family members and educators;
- Literacy programs should support families in ways that make sense to both parents and children;
- We must honor, validate, and use the languages of the parents and children who are enrolled in our schools and who participate in our family literacy programs;
- All public policy regarding families and literacy should begin with the shared understanding that families have a right define themselves;
- Families and communities have the right to voice their concerns, influence policy, and set agendas at local, national, and international levels.

Heinemann published the Declaration of Family Literacy Principles in 1998 in a book entitled *Many Families Many Literacies: An International Declaration of Principles*, with contributions from the scholars who participated as well as from family literacy practitioners around the world and from family members who were participants in family literacy programs. In 2000 *Many Families Many Literacies* was included in *Family Literacy: An Annotated Bibliography*, published by the U.S. Department of Education, Office of Educational Research and Improvement, and the National Institute on Early Childhood Development and Education.

MANY FAMILIES, MANY LITERACIES

Edited by Denny Taylor

AN INTERNATIONAL DECLARATION OF PRINCIPLES

"In 2000 Many Families Many Literacies was included in Family Literacy: An Annotated Bibliography, published by the U.S. Department of Education, Office of Educational Research and Improvement, and the National Institute on Early Childhood Development and Education

Many Families Many Literacies

A One-Year Document Analysis Revealed the Political Campaign to Change the Minds of Parents About How Children Learn to Write.

BEGINNING TO READ AND THE SPIN DOCTORS OF SCIENCE
THE POLITICAL CAMPAIGN TO CHANGE AMERICA'S MIND ABOUT HOW CHILDREN LEARN TO READ
NATIONAL COUNCIL OF TEACHERS OF ENGLISH (1998)

At the time of the international conference on families and literacies in Tucson in 1997, other events were taking place directly related to Denny Taylor's research and advocacy for children and family literacy. The teachers with whom she had worked in New Hampshire were under siege from far right groups promoting phonics and direct instruction programs. One of the elementary schools that had reduced the dropout rate in high school to single digit percentage points received such intense pressure to adhere to reductionist policy mandates that the principal and many of the teachers left the school. It was at this time that Phyllis Schlafly and Samuel Blumenfeld gained national attention for their promotion of phonics, and the Texas Business Round Table joined the cause when George Bush, who was then Governor of Texas, ran for president.

For the next year Denny Taylor embarked on an in-depth analysis of research studies undertaken by NICHD that were funded by McGraw-Hill, the publisher of the Open Court Basal Reading Program. Based on a document analysis of the reporting of this research in the media, one of the findings of this research was Denny Taylor's clear articulation of the multiple ways in which both scholars and journalists advanced a corporate friendly agenda. But the most provocative of her findings was that both in the research design and execution, the McGraw-Hill funded NICHD research on early reading instruction was unfairly biased in favor of McGraw-Hill's Open Court/Direct Instruction treatment group. She also provided documentary evidence that some of the key results of the study were misrepresented in favor of the Open Court/Direction Instruction treatment group. The peer reviewed research was published in 1998 by the National Council of Teachers of English in a book entitled: *Beginning to Read and the Spin Doctors of Science*, and with the subtitle: *The Political Campaign to Change America's Mind about How Children Learn to Write*.

One of the reasons *Beginning to Read and the Spin Doctors of Science* is still of importance for educators and the public is that it is in this book that Denny Taylor systematically documents the beginnings of the corporate education reform movement in both the U.S. and the U.K., that emphasizes transmission of skills approaches to instruction, high stakes testing, and the shift from public to private charter schools. Essentially, *Beginning to Read and the Spin Doctors of Science* provides insights into current public education policies and mandates that directly contradict the Declaration of Family Literacy Principles, which scholars from around the work developed during their participation in the working conference Denny Taylor organized when she was at the University of Arizona.

It is worth noting that in addition to her teaching commitments at the university, her research activism to establish a declaration of family literacy principals, and her research and writing that challenged the research conducted by NICHD and McGraw-Hill, Denny Taylor took advantage of her four years at the University of Arizona to take advanced courses and seminars in sociolinguistics and psycholinguistics. These studies deepened these aspects of her transdisciplinary scholarship, which also included advanced graduate studies in anthropology, psychology, sociology and education. Her personal quest has always been to gain new insights into the human condition – the indomitable courage of families to take care of their children, and the proclivity of governments to behave in ways that are deleterious to children. Families, language, literacy and learning continue to be the organizing principles of her scholarship, but it was at this time that violence and trauma became more central to her thinking and to the future fieldwork she would undertake.

BEGINNING TO READ AND THE SPIN DOCTORS OF SCIENCE
NATIONAL COUNCIL OF TEACHERS OF ENGLISH (1998)

1998-2013: The Establishment of A New Literacy Studies Department and Doctoral Programs in Literacy Studies with an Emphasis on Family Literacy at Hofstra University.

CREATING CARING LITERACY COMMUNITIES
WAS A HIGH PRIORITY IN THE DEVELOPMENT OF
THE MASTERS AND DOCTORAL PROGRAMS

Occasionally during these years of research and writing Denny Taylor was invited to consider endowed chairs at leading universities. She consistently declined. But in 1998 she was invited to apply for a position at Hofstra University that would provide her with an opportunity to create a department and doctoral program almost from scratch. In 1998 she accepted this offer and relocated to Long Island, New York. She entered Hofstra University to take up the challenge of building a new Department of Literacy Studies and creating a new Doctoral Program in Literacy Studies. It was only the third time in the history of the university that a scholar had entered the institution as a full professor with tenure, and the first time a scholar with no prior formal academic experience had been invited to establish a new graduate department and create two completely new doctoral degree programs. It was only the third time in the history of the university that a scholar had entered the institution as a full professor with tenure, and the first time a scholar with no prior formal academic experience had been invited to establish a new graduate department and create two completely new doctoral degree programs.vv

During these early years at Hofstra, Denny Taylor spoke frequently of her commitment to shared governance, and together with the faculty and students she established their mission to use literacy to create caring communities both at the university and in schools and communities. Her efforts to enhance the opportunities for both faculty and students to think about language, literacy and learning were always transdisciplinary. "Don't ask me to think!" a masters student once said to her. "Tell me what to do" – and Denny Taylor replied, "What I want

PHOTO
Denny Taylor and Doctoral Students at the University of Pennsylvania Ethnographic Conference February 29th 2008. Left - Right: Erica Pecorale, Denny Taylor, Denise Yee-Vignola, Bobbie Kabuto, David Schultz

you to do is think."

With the support of the faculty and administration she embraced her new leadership role in the reconceptualization – philosophical, theoretical and conceptual frameworks – of eleven advanced degree programs. All of the courses in every degree program were rewritten. Enrollment doubled during this time period. By 2003 there were approximately 300 M.A. and M.S. students and 40 Ph.D. and Ed.D. students. Among the courses that Denny Taylor personally developed are the following:

- Apprenticeship in the Ethnography of Literacy Research;
- Advanced Seminar in the Ethnography of Literacy Research;
- The Ethnographic Imagination: Existentialism, Empiricism, and the Philosophy of Mind;
- Works and Influence of Mikhail Bakhtin;
- Sociolinguistics and Psycholinguistics Research Seminar;
- Family, Community, and School Literacies: Cultural Perspectives;
- Family, Community, School and Workplace Literacy;
- Literacy Learning at Home and in School: Social Contexts of Young Children Learning to Read and Write;
- Children and Adolescents as Ethnographers in Communities and Schools;
- Literacy, Art, Music and Dance (undergraduate and graduate courses);
- Writing Pictures, Painting Stories as Mindful Social Practice.

While maintaining her research and writing, Denny Taylor also supported the research and writing of faculty and students, often presenting with them at international and national conferences. Her work with doctoral students and as chair of their dissertation committees invariably led to presentations and publications – both scholarly articles and many books. She enthusiastically fostered scholarly connections with other universities, and she developed a Distinguished Visiting Scholar Series. Visiting professors from four continents and many countries included renowned anthropologists, sociologists, and linguists, as well as an M.D. with a specialty in neurology and a Ph.D. in linguistics.

Parenthetically, it was at this time of intense local, national and international community development at Hofstra that Denny Taylor was inducted into the International Reading Association's (now ILA) Reading Hall of Fame, which has approximately 100 members worldwide of renowned scholars in the fields of language, literacy and learning. In her acceptance speech at the IRA's convention she presented the first set of graphics on the social contexts of children's language, literacy and learning in home and school settings. These graphics have become a signature of her academic research with transdisciplinary graphics developed depicting the systemic complexity of, for example, the impact of climate change and related disasters on human societies worldwide. A selection of these transdisciplinary graphics is presented in the accompanying appendices.

Twenty-Two International Scholars Forums on Children, Literacy, Learning and Mass Trauma.

THESE TRANSDISCIPLINARY FORUMS BROUGHT TO HOFSTRA
WORLD CLASS SCHOLARS WHO ARE ACTIVISTS AND ADVOCATES
AND WHO STRUGGLE AGAINST RACISM AND DISCRIMINATION

In her effort to create contexts for new thinking about children, literacy and learning she organized a series of 22 International Scholars Forums at Hofstra that brought to the university world-class scholars and humanistic researchers, who have shaped our thinking and are actively engaged in the struggle against discriminatory practices in all aspects of everyday life. Three International Scholars Forums are highlighted here because of the close connection they have with Denny Taylor's fieldwork in regions of armed conflict and catastrophic events, which is discussed below. The first forum took place eleven days after September 11th 2001. Four world-renowned women scholars with almost 350 years of research and teaching experience between them were the invited speakers at the forum. Margaret Meek Spencer, who was 79 years of age, was a passenger on one of the first transatlantic flights to arrive at Kennedy Airport after 9-11. Maxine Greene, who was 84 years of age, Louise Rosenblatt who was 96, and Yetta Goodman who was the youngest at 70, all traveled to Hofstra for the forum. The book *Great Women Scholars*, documenting their participation in the forum includes the following paragraphs in the introduction:

> On September 20th 2001, nine days after the Twin Towers fell, Margaret flew from London to New York on her own. The plane was empty except for twenty passengers who sat in silence as they reached New York and looked down into the crater seven floors deep and saw

the smoke rising from the twisted metal and rubble. At 79 years of age it was an act of courage when most did not feel courageous. She gave us hope when we were not hopeful. Louise Rosenblatt, Maxine Greene and Yetta Goodman did the same. It is not possible to talk about the historic moment when these four great women met at an International Scholars Forum at Hofstra University without talking about September 11. ...

Without naming what we did we spent our time re-examining our thoughts and beliefs, re-describing our work as activists and advocates, reinventing ourselves as teachers and scholars. We explored the ethical stances that we take, our philosophical beliefs and pedagogical practices. From the intricate recesses of our personhood, ideas that had become part of our identity, part of our consciousness, so much so that we had taken ownership, became available to us in ways that we had not anticipated.

The second forum of note took place in 2005, and focused on using literacy to support children who have experienced armed conflict or natural disasters. Participants included researchers, M.D's. and human rights activists from Sri Lanka, South Africa, Rwanda, Israel, and Palestine, as well as researchers from the UK and across the United States.

The third forum of note was on children, literacy and trauma, and took place in 2007. Public school teachers, who had become first responders when Hurricane Katrina destroyed their homes, communities and schools, were the featured speakers. At the time of the forum many teachers including some of the presenters, were still living in trailers. First responders, Doris Voitier (superintendent of schools), Aretha Williams (principal), Carole Mundt and Christine Karn (teachers), and Cindy Elliott (professor) all participated in the forum, and more will be written about their courageous response to Hurricane Katrina below.

PHOTO
Gaza Children, 2003

The International Center for Everybody's Child (ICEC) at Hofstra University.

ICEC SUPPORTED CHILDREN WHEN CATASTROPHIC EVENTS OCCURRED
AND PROVIDED SUSTAINABLE ASSISTANCE WHEN ON-GOING
EMERGENCIES OCCURRED

The impact of 9-11 on the community in which Denny Taylor was living, and in the communities in which her graduate students were teaching, had a profound effect on her thinking about children, literacy, and mass trauma. She became critically conscious that it is not only when catastrophic events take place that children are traumatized, but also that living in urban and rural communities where there is extreme poverty can be traumatic -- not only for individual children and adults but for whole communities.

It was this understanding that became the driving force in Denny Taylor's establishment of the International Center for Everybody's Child (ICEC) at Hofstra University. With the support of the Provost Herman Berliner, she created and directed the center known as ICEC, and it was the center that co-sponsored the 2005 and 2007 forums mentioned above.

The central premise of ICEC was that for the common good of *all* children it is essential that we share knowledge, increase understanding and improve the educational opportunities, irrespective of the children's race, ethnicity, gender, religion or national identity.

The research focus of ICEC was on children, literacy, trauma, and peace, with an emphasis on the impact of weather related and ecological catastrophes and sociopolitical disasters including armed conflict on the lives of children, their families and communities. One of the major research questions was:

> If we include consideration for the health and well-being of everybody's child in our response to the global crises that are taking place, how would that affect our present and future actions?

This is one of the questions that runs through the entire 40 years of Denny Taylor's research and continues to frame her research to the present day. The question necessitated at ICEC new ways of thinking about the interconnections between the social, psychological, biological, and physical sciences to:

- Increase the social and psychological resources and educational opportunities provided to children;
- Strengthen their resiliency of children and their families to provide opportunities for them to recover from traumatic experiences;
- Engage children in activities created to support their emotional and physical well-being as well as enhance their academic development and access to literacy.

ICEC provided many opportunities for teachers in the U.S. and from around the world who were working in areas of extreme poverty, regions of armed conflict and natural disasters to meet with peace workers, humanitarian aid professionals, and trauma specialists to share experiences and develop first response initiatives. Participants included survivors of the Rwandan genocide, and peace workers and teachers responding to armed conflict in Israel, the West Bank and Gaza.

The idea was to create new kinds of international professional communities and social organizations that can work together for the collective good of children and their families who live not only in remote parts of the world, but also in the U.S. in such places as Louisiana and Mississippi, where children and their families received inadequate support following the devastation and loss of their homes, schools and communities due to

Hurricanes Katrina and Rita.

It was at this time that Denny Taylor wrote:

My hope is that in the coming years we will develop collaborative initiatives in the US and international partnerships to increase the social and psychological resources and educational opportunities of children to strengthen their resiliency and recovery from trauma. This work must be local as well as global and have a multidisciplinary focus on the life sustaining needs and educational opportunities of children who live in areas of extreme poverty and public health emergencies, places of conflict or post conflict, and parts of the world in which there are natural and social disasters.

Emphasis must be on the importance of the re-establishment of schools following catastrophic events, and the importance of long term educational opportunities for children who have experiences of emergency situations. We must develop pedagogical practices in safe environments, which focus on using language and literacy activities, and arts and science projects, to create joyful classrooms and schools. These activities and projects must be culturally and linguistically relevant and build on the strengths of the children. Above all they must be meaningful to the children who have experienced traumatic events or are experiencing ongoing adverse events.

At ICEC emphasis was placed on the resistance of cultural imposition and the importance of local teachers' voices and narratives. Recognition was also given to the importance of connecting with conflicting groups and the acceptance of irreconcilable narratives of the same lived events. Importance was placed on the exploration of commonalities in teaching and learning across cultural contexts, and sustaining local teachers and teaching organizations through the use of technology to connect them with teachers and scholars in the international community.

The purpose and intent of ICEC were ambitious, but Denny Taylor was convinced by her many years of research with vulnerable communities and in regions of armed conflict and catastrophic events that it was entirely possible, and the urgency of the work and for the center is unquestionable. She expressed the urgency of these efforts as follows:

We must try to influence what is happening to children. Remember what Louise Rosenblatt said at the Great Women's Scholars Forum just after 9-11.

"No matter what your gender, your race, your religion, every child is entitled to life, liberty and the pursuit of happiness that does not harm others."

In her one hundred and first year, up until the time she died, Louise lobbied the U.S. Congress on behalf of children and their teachers.

"Those who sit back and wait, are, I believe, ignoring children whose lives are affected," Louise Rosenblatt wrote. "We must try to influence what is happening to children, and if we fail, as well we may, we shall at least have spread some ideas, have educated some, who will continue the resistance."

So many of my friends, the ones I know and the ones I read are a part of this struggle. Young or old, beginning or retiring and continuing to work, I smile when I think of them. This is an extraordinary time to be in the company of teachers. For longer than we can remember teachers have been working for the dissolution of human divides, crossing borders and mending rifts.

PHOTO
Child participating in a Family Literacy Night organized by graduate students in LYST 212 at Hofstra

Children and Armed Conflict: Theoretical Understandings Should Be Informed by Lived Experience.

THE GREATEST DISCOVERY THAT WE COULD MAKE
IS HOW TO ENSURE THE SURVIVAL OF OUR CHILDREN

Denny Taylor's conviction that theoretical understandings should be informed by lived experiences led her to undertake a series of fieldwork experiences in a region of armed conflict. One of her doctoral students, whose dissertation research was conducted in an elementary school in Tel Aviv arranged for Denny Taylor to visit schools in Tel Aviv and in West and East Jerusalem. It was at this time that she wrote:

> The greatest discovery that human beings could make in the 21st century is how to ensure the survival of their children. It's a discovery that will necessitate the dissolution of racial and ethnic divides, crossing national and cultural borders, and mending religious and political rifts. Scientists in every field, discipline and paradigm would need to work together with physicians, politicians, business leaders and philanthropists. This is unlikely to happen but for longer than we can remember teachers have been working for the dissolution of human divides, crossing borders and mending rifts. There is much we can learn from them.

Networking before leaving the United States and also when she arrived in Israel, Denny Taylor made arrangements to also visit the West Bank, and she was invited to stay in the home of a Palestinian teacher in Ramallah. In a paper, entitled *Terror-Eyes and Terrorized* she writes of both Israeli and Palestinian children's experiences of armed conflict and violence. It is now 14 years since she wrote the paper and the passages that follow are the only excerpts of the paper in the public domain, because of her concern at the time for the safety of the teachers and young people with whom she'd met. In the introduction she wrote:

> In March 2003 the hotel in which I am staying is filled with U.S. military of high rank. They are loud, brash and invasive. I watch President Bush on CNN. "We are overcoming darkness with the light of hope," he says as Arafat, Qaddafi, and Saddam Hussein flash across the screen. "Whose darkness?" I write in my notebook. "Whose hope?"

> I am travelling between Tel Aviv, Jerusalem and Ramallah meeting with teachers and visiting schools. It's quiet in my hotel room. I'm no longer watching CNN. In a letter that I brought with me from New York, Maxine Greene, the philosopher, writes of her interest in "wide-awakeness," "thoughtfulness" and of "breaking somehow through the walls of confusion, manipulation and media control." In the letter she has included lines from a poem by Adrienne Rich:

> > If I withdraw from seeing and if I withdraw
> >
> > from engaging myself in this confusion
> >
> > if only for myself
> >
> > what am I?

> ...When I meet him in Tel Aviv a professor at a teachers college calls the principal in a school I had visited "a cul-

tural hero." He tells me about the participation of the students from the college at the school and of their work with the caregivers of the preschool children of the foreign workers. He speaks of humanism before nationalism, humanistic morality, social democracy, and equal rights for the Arabs in Israel. "If you are a humanist you are there for every human being and not those just of your tribe," he says, making it clear how difficult it is to separate the rights of children from politics or religion.

I talk about my research on children and war. "What was the impact of the explosions on the children at the school?" I ask.

"The trauma was seeing the parts of the body on the street," he explains. "Because one of the frightening things is that after such an attack if you go to the street you see a head here, a foot here and probably some of the children saw things like this. Butchery. That's what bothers the children the most. But relatively, children here can enjoy life, day by day. I mean it's only once or twice they suffer from a terror attack."

"It's much, much worse for the Palestinians now," he continues. "If I can evaluate the situation of the children in the West Bank, it's much worse," he says. "What they go through just seeing their parents and their grandparents humiliated day by day by soldiers and losing one brother after another, it's totally different."

"You see," he explains, "You can have one trauma, a second trauma, a third trauma, but the Palestinians have been under occupation for more than fifty years. And especially for the last two or three years, they have been under bombardment and attack almost every day. It's total madness. Totally insane."

"We must make every effort to make Israel more humanistic," he tells me. He speaks of the need for "reconciled dialogues" and "other narratives." He says, "If a teacher comes to class with the intention of discussing a social issue, the children stop the discussion. The children are totally intolerant. They terrorize the teacher. Students shout, 'Kill the Arabs! Kill the Arabs!' We often read of the children of Arabs hating us. Now it's our children who hate."

The professor quotes Camus and speaks of "the plague we bring on ourselves." Again he helps me understand how difficult it is to keep the focus on children without addressing the political. Speaking of teachers he says, "We are the party that criticizes the suffering of children." Then just before I leave he says, "If the focus is on children, definitely the situation where the army, the military, closes schools and universities, that's inhumane." ...

In New York I have been given the name of a Palestinian teacher that I can contact when I arrive in Israel. "Come," the Palestinian teacher tells me when I call him in Ramallah from the hotel Tel Aviv. "It will be okay."

When I reach the checkpoint the taxi driver, who is an Israeli Palestinian, agrees to meet me at four the next day. He tells me there is often shooting at night and to make sure I am back before dark. "Follow those women," he says, as I get out of the car. I walk as if I do this every day, as if I know where I am going and know who I am meeting, even though I do not. People are shouting. "Keep walking," a man says as he passes me, "don't stop, look down." I can see soldiers. I make my way towards them, between concrete dividers and barbed wire, stepping through the debris and on sandbags sunk in the mud. One of the soldiers looks at me but does not speak and I

PHOTO
Gaza City, 2003: Children's art incorporating artillery casings picked up by children in the playground

walk on. The noise fades even though I can still hear people are shouting. I am between one place and another, nowhere not somewhere, and I am aware that the light is fading. ...

The noise increases. Taxis. Vans. "Ram!" Ram!" Drivers shout in a language I do not understand. I know nothing about this place and it is getting dark. People walk quickly, move slowly, and stand still. I can see a man and a boy waving, smiling, and I smile and wave too, for the circumstances have made us old friends even though this is the first time we have met. ...

When I visit the Minister of Education with the teacher with whom I am staying he talks about the invasion of the Ministry of Education, and the destruction of all their data banks and computers. He speaks of school closures because of frequent curfews ...

"When schools are closed parents organize schools in mosques," the teacher says. "No one knows what they are teaching them. It's a huge problem."

"It's not in our hands," the Minister says. "Even when children are in school it is out of our hands. How can we work to remove the hatred from the hearts of our students?"

On this point there is agreement between the Palestinian Minister of Education and the Israeli professor at the teacher's college who I visited. Palestinian and Israeli children are growing up hating each other and schools are having difficulty dealing with the problem. In Tel Aviv children are terrified, their eyes filled with fear. In Ramallah the eyes of the children are filled with dread. Terrorized and with terror-eyes, many Israeli and Palestinian children have seen their friends die and members of their families are dead.

"After the invasion," the teacher with whom I am staying says, "it was necessary to do crisis management to keep the schools open and to keep the teachers and children going." He speaks of "thinking loudly," rather than "brain storming" and says that, because of the invasion and occupation, schools are filled with children who have "remarkable special needs." During the last two years of Israeli occupation the injuries of more than 500 children have resulted in permanent disabilities.

"We are trying to create an atmosphere in which everyone is welcome in our schools," he says, and he talks about the work his non-profit organization is doing to establish cooperative learning environments. He explains that children learn English in first grade, and that between curfews and soldiers' occupation of schools he works with teachers on the democratization of the curriculum.

"Our main concern is to create a secure environment for learning," the Minister of Education states, "but it's difficult when the children are thinking about the invasion, the checkpoints, and about getting back safely to their homes." He is visibly distressed, "How can I justify my life as a human being when so many children are being killed?"

The teacher talks of the right of every child to be nurtured and protected.

"War is not a game for Palestinian children," he says, as he talks of children experiencing severe psychological and emotional problems and of their inability to concentrate in school. "They are frightened," he says, "they worry that the soldiers will come back and they will not be able to reach their homes."

... In a high school I talk with eleventh grade students, two young men and one young woman.

"We want to tell people how we live here," one says. "We are always suffering," says another. They speak in English and I record the conversation. "It used to take me ten minutes to come to school now it takes me hours. And during the curfews no one can get out of his house." "Everyone stays in and we miss education. What is that supposed to do?" "We stay in our homes three days, four days, one month, you can't go out."

"They take our lives, any time they want." "It's not knowing what is going to happen next. We don't know what is going to happen tomorrow. Not being able to come to school, not being able to do anything, not having the right to live next month." "They put us under stress." "Fear." "We want to live, we are so lucky that we still have hope." "We *can* live." "We *want* to live." "We want to live with our dignity. We want to have a life. Go to school."

"We just want the American people to see the truth. Not to be with us or anything but just to see what is really happening." "Not to believe CNN and all the American media, 24 Hours. When twenty children die here they say it on the news like nothing is happening. That's what is so unfair." "Yes. There is no fair media. You have to come here and see the real situation not the media. The media lies."

"They think we like to die, kill ourselves, and kill them. But they don't think why did that person kill himself? Why did he go there? He lost his brother. He lost his mother. What made him do this? They think he is a terrorist. All Palestinians are terrorists."

"But the real reason for killing himself is for giving his people more hope." "Palestinians want to make peace, but not this peace." "We are living under occupation. We are the last country in the world to be occupied."

"Imagine yourself you can't go anywhere. You can't do anything except go to school, not every day because of the curfews. It's horrible. Nobody in the whole world can imagine that, I think."

Denny Taylor returned to Israel and the West Bank in July 2003. She visited with families and schools in Israel and once again stayed with the teacher and his family in Ramallah. On this visit she also stayed with a family in the refugee camp at Raffah visiting schools and families after entering Gaza at the Erez military checkpoint. After three attempts to cross she was given permission and she was allowed entrance even though the crossing had been closed to civilians for more than three months. Other visits to the region followed with Denny Taylor staying in the homes of Palestinian families and visiting more schools in Gaza and West Bank towns and villages.

Denny Taylor's conviction that theoretical understandings should be informed by lived experiences led her to undertake a series of fieldwork experiences in a region of armed conflict.

Integrating Knowledge of PTSD and Other Psychiatric Sequelae of Trauma as it Applies to the Approach to First Response Initiative in the Aftermath of Disaster.

TEACHERS ARE OFTEN FIRST RESPONDERS
BUT THEY ARE NOT MEDICAL PROFESSIONALS AND
MUST BE SUPPORTED

Increasingly her scholarship focused on children, literacy, and mass trauma and she was mentored by a psychiatrist who was a survivor of a traumatic event that had left him a paralyzed and in intense pain but still teaching and meeting with patients. The purpose of this mentorship was Denny Taylor's in-depth study of the medical and psychoanalytic literature that focused on integrating knowledge of PTSD and other psychiatric sequelae of trauma as they apply to the psychiatric approach in the aftermath of disaster. She also attended conferences organized by the Medical Society of the State of New York on the psychological impact of disaster and terrorism and Grand Rounds at the hospital where the psychiatrist was affiliated on those occasions when the focus was children and mass trauma.

For Denny Taylor the intent was to add new ways of looking and thinking to the transdisciplinary approach to research that she continued to build, while at the same time assisting her in the development of guidelines for teachers who were often first responders in regions of armed conflict and when catastrophic events occurred. The task was to develop guidelines that recognized that teachers are not medical practitioners or therapists, but that there is still much they can do (and not do) to care for children when events occur.

PHOTO
Aftermath of Hurricane Sandy, 2012

PHOTO
Aftermath of Armed Conflict

PHOTO
Aftermath of Sandy Hook, 2012

First Response Initiatives in the Immediate Aftermath of Hurricanes Katrina and Rita, and the Failure of the Levees.

THE RIVER CENTER IN BATON ROUGE BECAME A SHELTER FOR 5,000 PEOPLE
WHEN THE LEVEES BROKE IN THE AFTERMATH OF
THE DEVASTATING STORMS

When Hurricanes Katrina and Rita and the failure of the levees devastated the Gulf Region of Louisiana, Denny Taylor sent an email to the listserv for the Center for the Expansion of Language and Thinking (CELT) and she received an email from Cynthia Elliott at Southeastern Louisiana University asking her to come to Baton Rouge to assist teachers who were first responders working with children in the aftermath of the storm. Although Denny Taylor did not know Cindy Elliott she agreed and flew from New York to Baton Rouge the following day. In the weeks that followed Cindy Elliott and Denny Taylor provided guidance to teachers who had take up the role of first responders in eight schools in the Louisiana Parishes in the vicinity of New Orleans. However, when Denny Taylor first arrived in Baton Rouge, Cindy Elliott drove her directly to the River Center that had become a shelter for 5,000 people when the levees broke in the aftermath of the Katrina and Rita.

Denny Taylor made multiple visits to Louisiana in the aftermath of the Hurricanes. Here are two excerpts from her ethnographic notes:

"Help!" a little girl silently shouts. "Help!" She mouths the word but no sound comes out. She is sitting alone on a cot in the shelter at the River Center in Baton Rouge five weeks after Hurricanes Katrina and Rita. I stop and ask her if she is okay. She looks at me and nods. The pain in her eyes is distressing to see and I want to sit with her, but I am in a hurry. It's late and I've been told I must leave. I am trying to get medical assistance for Suzie, one of three sisters I've been visiting in the shelter. Suzie has Crohn's disease and she is a double amputee. She cannot eat the food in the shelter and her stumps are bleeding. I met Suzie and her sisters one week after Katrina. Their house was in New Orleans Parish in the section known as Lakeview. "Ground zero," Her sister Marianne called it.

"She has lesions on her stumps and they are bleeding," Suzie's other sister says.

"They're bleeding a lot," Suzie says. "They keep bleeding." She is sitting in her wheelchair, in one of the corners of the River Center with her sisters, just as she was when I first met her, but her face is now ashen and she looks so malnourished I'm visibly shaken. Diane and Marianne are looking at me. They are both haggard and there are dark circles beneath their eyes. …

Right now I am in a hurry to get medical help for Suzie. I bend down and speak to the little girl who has silently cried for help. The cots on either side of the one on which she is sitting are empty and there is no adult in her immediate vicinity. When I ask her if she is okay I know she is not. I tell her I'll come back and she looks at me as if she doesn't expect to see me again.

I pass the National Guard outpost eyes down, hoping that they will not kick me out. At the medical center a Red Cross volunteer tells me there are no doctors in the shelter and the medical center is closed. I tell the Red Cross volunteer about Suzie, that she has received no medical attention since she arrived at the shelter, that she has Crohn's, that she can't eat the food, that she is malnourished, and that her stumps are bleeding. Getting medical help takes time but I am determined. It's a complicated story, but eventually the Red Cross volunteer and a paramedic tell me that they will make sure a doctor sees her the following morning. The volunteer says she will do her best to have Suzie transferred to another facility. She says she will make sure her sisters go with her. I rush back to tell Suzie, Marianne and Diane, and on the way I try to find the little girl. I ask a woman lying on the cot next to the one on which the little girl had been sitting, but she says there aren't any children on the cots near to her. I look around but hurry on. It's important that the sisters know that the doctor will see Suzie, and I want to encourage them to take her to the medical center in the morning.

Three years after Hurricanes Katrina and Rita and the failure of the levees, Denny Taylor returned to Louisiana, and together with Cindy Elliott, she met with a group of teachers in St. Bernard Parish who had become first responders in the immediate aftermath of the catastrophic storms. Teachers talked of children still suffering and of children needing time to discuss what has happened to them during and after Katrina. Again, here are excerpts from Denny Taylor's ethnographic notes:

"Some children stayed and some saw death right in front of them," a teacher says.

"We came back on a Tuesday night," one of the teachers says telling her own story. "We moved into our trailer. That night my sister came banging on the door crying 'Daddy is dead.' He wasn't sick. I think he just couldn't rebuild again."

"One catastrophe can lead to another," a teacher says. She recounts, "A child holding on to a tree with his mother and father was coping okay, and then his mother tried to commit suicide."

"Catastrophes happen and children might cope," another teacher says, "but a year later, two years later, problems surface."

Three years after Hurricane Katrina, tragedies are still occurring. The psychiatrist Anand Pandya (2006) provides verification of the experiences of the Louisiana teachers when he speaks of the expectation of "symptoms" during the acute phase of an emergency that become "transient and fluid," often recurring weeks, months or years after the disaster happens. He speaks of the "let down," and so did the Louisiana teachers, who talked at length about the changes they were observing in their students' behaviors, as they began to understand that their families, schools and communities would never be the same as they were before Katrina.

The teachers talked of Katrina becoming part of children's identity.

"'Hi. I'm John and I was in Katrina,'" a teacher says.

"They live the storm," another says.

In the immediate aftermath of the Hurricane, Richard Robinson, the CEO and Chairman of Scholastic Inc., published *The Kate Middleton Elementary School: Portraits of Hope and Courage* in which Denny Taylor told the story of how the principal and teachers at the Kate Middleton Elementary School in Jefferson Parish cleared away all the debris from the storm and salvaged the parts of the school that were still habitable, and how they posted and handed out flyers in the community telling families that the school was reopening and that irrespective of whether they were on the register any child in the community was welcome to attend. Denny Taylor combined the story of Kate Middleton with practical advice derived from her research with teachers in Israel, the West Bank and Gaza to provide first response guidance for parents and teachers in the Gulf Region, as well as in schools across the country where evacuees were sent. Richard Robinson had 500,000 copies of this teachers-as-first-responders magazine published and he had them distributed to public schools across the United States.

Since that time she has made the first response guidelines available to all public schools in regions affected by catastrophic events, and she has organized forums taught courses, and given seminars for teachers as first responders in the aftermath of catastrophic events.

PHOTO
A teacher welcomes a kindergarten child on the first day of school in 2005 in the aftermath of Hurricanes Katrina and Rita and the failure of the levees

Responding to Catastrophic Events through Language and Literacy.

THE TASK FOR THE LITERACY RESEARCHER IS TO DOCUMENT THE IMMEDIATE AFTERMATH OF A DISASTER
AND THEN USE THE ANALYSIS OF THE DATA TO INFORM FIRST RESPONSE INITIATIVES

Denny Taylor was convinced that in times when catastrophic events take place, and when on-going emergency situations occur, language and literacy can also become organizing principles. It was at this time that she wrote in her notes:

> For researchers and educators of language and literacy the early development of this critical area of study draws on complementary and contradictory theories of language, literacy and learning and on medical research on trauma and mass trauma. In places of armed conflict or natural disasters, or in regions of extreme poverty, or public health emergencies it is essential that field based research juxtapose contested paradigms and metatheories, positivist and constructivist, Cartesian and post formal, and uses them within cultural contexts to support children whose lives have been disrupted by the events that are taking place. Serious work cannot be done without close collaboration with members of local communities, including local NGO's, and international humanitarian aid organizations, physicians and public health professionals.

When situated language and literacy practices become organizing principles, local languages and literacies provide multiple opportunities for researchers to gain in depth understandings of the social semiotic spaces that exist or have been socially constructed in the aftermath of the catastrophic event or in on-going emergency situation. In addition, through ethnographic research understandings of the social semiotic spaces that have been damaged or destroyed can also be gained. Recognition of the importance of local, regional, national, indigenous, colonial languages and writing systems and literacy practices is critical to the work. In such situations literacy researchers and educators work with other first responders who have different mandates and guidelines, different purposes and agendas, and different social and political identities.

The task for the literacy researcher and educators is to document the immediate aftermath of a disaster, and then to use the analysis of this documentation to work with other members of the local community and international aid organizations to support the reestablishment of social environments in which families live and children go to school. Learning more about the local conditions: housing, medical care, water, food, transportation, mobility, and communication are essential. Information about deaths and injuries of family members, and the separation of families is important. Living in the region of Middle East conflict a third grade child writes, "I miss my family. It's more than 20 months since last time I saw my grandma, aunts, uncles and cousins." In the River Center shelter in Baton Rouge three sisters look at pictures in a photograph album. It is one of the few possessions that they have left after the hurricane. "Two years ago Daddy died," one of the sisters said. "Then our little dog died and it snowed at Christmas in New Orleans." She turns the page. "I take a picture of this tree every year. I love this tree. Now it's gone. There's nothing left. It's all gone."

Thus in the aftermath of Hurricanes Katrina, Rita and the failure of the levees Denny Taylor began crossing borders into the physical sciences. These efforts required a steep learning curve and she spent several hours a day studying the science as it pertained to climate change and ecological disasters and, while she considered these efforts a high priority, another significant aspect of these experiences was that they encouraged the expansion of her transdisciplinary research.

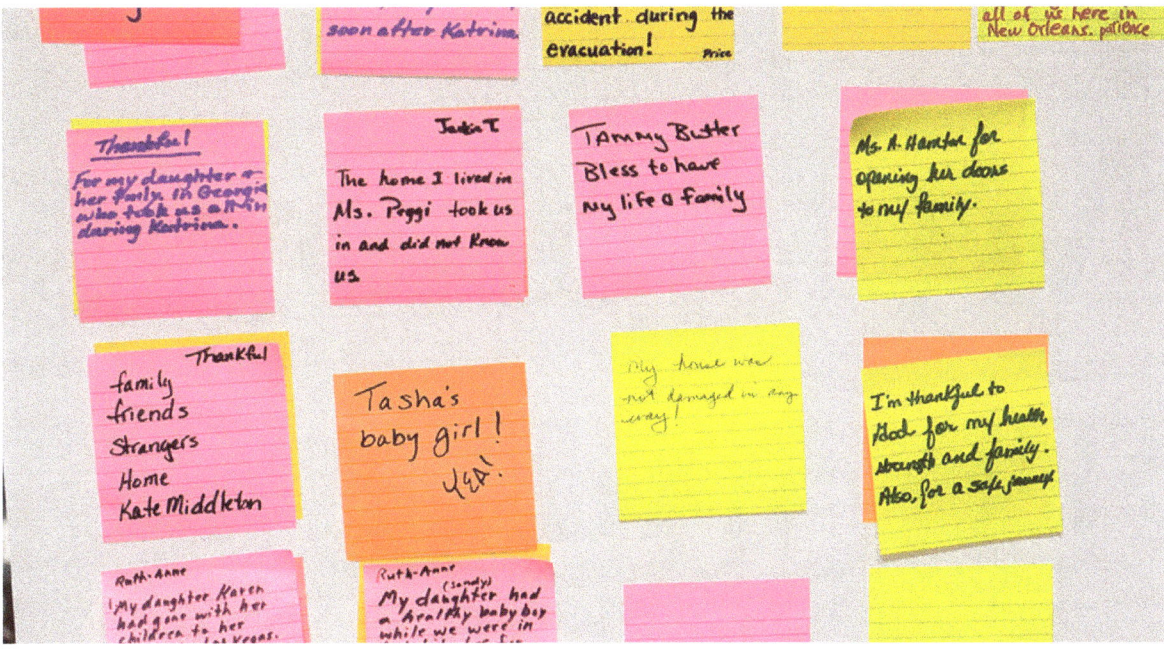

PHOTO
In the aftermath of Hurricanes Katrina and Rita teachers at the Kate Middleton School participated in first response activities before the school reopened and the children returned.

Families, Medicine, Empathy, and Metaphoric Thought.

ALL LANGUAGE IS EMBEDDED IN HUMAN EXPERIENCE
PEOPLE'S WAYS OF KNOWING CAN BE THEORETICALLY LOCATED IN THEIR SOCIAL ACTIONS

⟶

It was also at this time that Denny Taylor revisited previous studies reanalyzing the ethnographic data she had collected using new approaches to analysis that were emerging from her studies in the physical sciences. One such effort focused on the complex literacies that determined the life and death of a participant in the study that was published in the book *Toxic Literacies*. Laurie, a mother in the study for whom she became and advocate, was denied surgery for cervical cancer because she did not have health insurance and the decision was made to irradiate the cancer and Laurie subsequently died.

Using graphic representations Denny Taylor was able to show the disparities between the ways of thinking of the hospital personnel and doctors and Laurie's ways of thinking as the patient. Together, the two graphics were entitled *Families, Medicine, Empathy, and Metaphoric Thought*.

The first graphic presented from the perspective of doctors and public health profession an analysis of the social construction of communicative practices of a medical emergency. This graphic included: cultural historical, political, biological/physical, psychological/cognitive, psychological/emotional and social perspectives. The second graphic presented an analysis of the situated communicative practices constitutive of the medical emergency from the perspective of the patient. This graphic included: semiotic, semantic, modalities, discourse, pragmatics, and physical space perspectives.

Among the theoretical assumptions underlying all of Denny

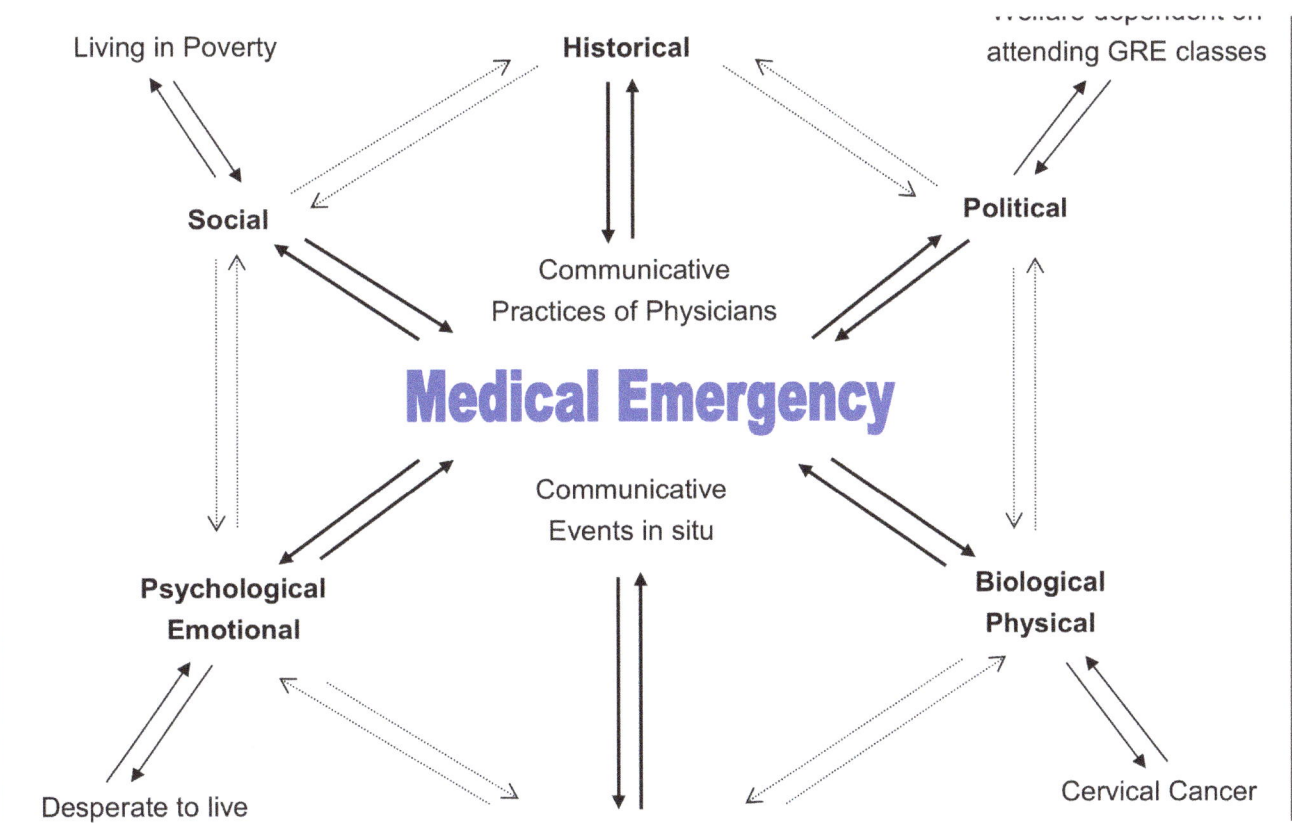

PHOTO
The Social Construction of a Medical Emergency Communicative Practices and Events

Taylor's graphic representations of the interrelationships between the social and physical world are the following:

- All thought is metaphoric;
- All language is embedded in human experience;
- Communication is more than information processing;
- Language is used to identify the world, is part of ongoing action, is used to represent thoughts and feelings, and is used to construct relationships;
- People's ways of knowing can be theoretically located in their social interactions, revealing their biological, cultural, social, historical, national, philosophical, religious, and political engagement in the world through metaphoric thought;
- Stressful life experiences can impair the possibilities of metaphoric thought and empathetic knowing, forming a stumbling block to communication that has far-reaching consequences for families, children and society;
- The challenge is to become critically conscious of the profound need for reified (fixed) metaphoric thought to open-up to possibilities of empathetic ways of knowing and communicating.

For many years she had become concerned about the observable separation of the physical world from the dominant frameworks of family life and the human psyche. Again her concern was for children who were spending less and less time playing in or studying the natural world.

Shifts in societal norms associated with the corporate shift in public education eliminated the opportunities for these connections to be sustained, and ethnographic studies by Denny Taylor's students provided evidence that families had less and less time for engagement in activities that connected children with their environment.

The Re-Engagement of Families and Communities in Public Conversations About the Inseparable Relationships Between People and the Planet.

HOW LONG CAN THE EARTH SYSTEM SUSTAIN THE PRESENT RATE OF HUMAN INDUCED GLOBAL ENVIRONMENTAL CHANGE?
THIS IS AN EXISTENTIAL QUESTION

⟶

Drawing on all her previous work Denny Taylor focused her research efforts on ways to encourage the re-engagement of families and communities in public conversations about the inseparable relationships between people and the planet. This transdisciplinary research on the re-integration of humanity with nature combines perspectives from pre-17th century traditions with rapidly changing present day scientific views on people and the planet, which embrace ambiguity and theories of systemic complexity, and challenge the legacy of Descartes and the quest for certainty in 21st century societies.

Crossing fields, disciplines and paradigms, and working with different scales of documentation, she embarked on a transdisciplinary research initiative, which drew on the physical and social sciences and humanities in response to the overwhelming scientific evidence that people are changing the planet.

In one iteration of this work on the systemic complexity of the rapid changes taking place to the planet and to human societies, Denny Taylor developed a series of graphic representations depicting five theoretically and scientifically grounded conceptual metaphors: 1) *The Anthropocene*; 2) *Kicks*; 3) *Dead Zones*; 4) *The Great Acceleration*; and 5) *Bridging the Abyss*. Each metaphoric representation draws on the humanities as well as the sciences, and each descriptor embedded in the graphic representations is supported by an analysis of the key research within specific fields and disciplines across the social and physical sciences. Thus each conceptual metaphor that is graphically represented is constructed to address head-on the issues of resilience, vulnerability, adaptation, and transformation across the biophysical and social dimensions of anthropogenic global change.

Denny Taylor describes the visual representations as *useful fictions* – an attempt to depict the interactions of phenomena, occurring on multiple temporal and spatial scales, happening both simultaneously and sequentially, that are contingent and conditional, and are highly dependent on the interactions of many other phenomena that have taken place, from deep time stretching through the present time and into the future.

Each Conceptual Metaphor:

- Combines the physical, biological, and social sciences with the humanities;
- Includes data from governmental, economic, and industrial sources, as well as social media;
- Provides transdisciplinary spaces that encourage situated engagement in research on climate change, biodiversity loss, ecosystem degradation *with* research on the impact of human enterprise on the planet as well as research on human vulnerability and resiliency;
- Encourages the global science community to find new approaches to engage political leaders, government establishments, and the public sector—to prevent, mitigate, adapt and transform— but most importantly to act.

By 2008 Denny Taylor was submitting research proposals to present at international conferences organized by climate scientists and researchers across the physical sciences. In August 2009 she participated in the ICSU/ISSC On-Line Global Visioning Consultation that had 1,016 registered users from 85 countries, and during which 323 research questions were posed which were used as a basis for a document on the Grand Challenges

PHOTO
Using new technologies parents and children can expand their worlds, gaining access to social and scientific resources, which underscore the complexity of life and the separable relationships between people and the planet

facing humanity. In her notes in response to the event Denny Taylor wrote:

> The questions posted during the on-line visioning ranged from the carefully formulated to the quickly written with scientists writing in English to and for each other at a time when they are under intense scrutiny. Many scientists in the physical sciences have been personally threatened and so some participated in the on-line visioning identifying themselves only by their first names or no names at all.

"How long can the Earth system sustain the present rate of human-induced global-environmental change?" one scientist asks in Question 23. "Humans are modifying the planet at an alarming rate," he continues. "The critical question is how long can planetary environmental processes continue to function before these human-induced changes trigger negative feedbacks that result in a switch to an alternate and less supportive Earth system state?"

"This to me is the pressing question above all others," a participant responds.

"The Earth system is a self-regulated system," writes another, "we can only predict, forecast and try to mitigate the situation related with human-induced global-environmental change, but precise assessment on how long can the system sustain (human-induced global-environmental change) cannot be done."

The questions, narratives and responses also reflect a pervasive concern about the impact and existential risks of human-induced change on vulnerable people and communities.

"How can research help address the vicious circle of environmental change, resource scarcity, poverty, and poor health?" a scientist asks in Question 5. The scientist writes, "The Brundtland Report (WCED 1987, 27) stated '[m]any parts of the world are caught in a vicious downward spiral: poor people are forced to overuse environment further impoverishing them, making their survival ever more uncertain and difficult.' This statement and other aspects of the report have been debated for 20 years. The question, posed slightly differently here, remains one of the fundamental unsolved challenges for human-environment relations."

"The Brundtland statement is correct," a scientist responds, "but it sounds cynical if you fail to notice the excessive and heedless exploitation of our planet by mighty multinational corporations, and the often undifferentiated reflection about the reasons for poverty on the planet."

"I think the interdisciplinary problems," another scientist writes, "involving such issues as environmental change, resource scarcity, poverty, and poor health are among the most challenging problems a researcher can face … In Sub-Saharan Africa for instance, you can't carry out a research on environmental change without considering poverty alleviation, and human health improvement."

There is also a pervasive sense of urgency in the scientists' need to learn more about the complexity of the human-environmental dynamic.

"What is the role of land-use change for the present, past, and future evolution of the Earth?" a scientist, identified as "Chris", asks in Question 4.

"In addressing this question," Johan Bodegard, the Director of the Swedish Species Information Centre, responds. "I believe there is an urgent need to significantly improve our knowledge of the composition of ecosystems, e.g. species and genetic composition, as well as the functions of ecosystem processes."

"In order to understand the role of land use on global climate change in general and regional climate in particular," a scientist, identified as "ywoyessa", writes. "I believe it is important to understand the human-environment dynamics, the driving forces responsible for land use change and the socio-hydrological interactions."

"The huge ecological footprint of man on the land needs to be understood and reduced urgently," R.J. Thomas responds.

"Science is tasked with leading the way in changing itself," Andrew Fynn writes. "The benefits will expand beyond the successful resolution of the climate crisis. It's time to reinvent ourselves and reexamine the origins of science for clues to our future. Climate change reveals the disconnected nature of various pools of human talent, resources and endeavors. In order to overcome the unprecedented challenge of climate change we must break down the walls and learn how our institutions and mindsets need to change so that all branches of human endeavor are coordinated into one effective body." Fynn imagines "a vision of science that resides within the global community, not apart from the realities of life".

It is this vision of science residing in the global community and not apart from the realities of life that drives Denny Taylor to continue her reimagining of the relationships between the physical and social sciences and the humanities, even though she considers the task ahead is monumental and her own participation in this life-sustaining planetary endeavor is of very little significance at all.

In 2010 Denny Taylor participated in the ICSU/ISSC Open Visioning Consultation Forum, UNESCO, Paris, that resulted in the publication of the Grand Challenges Report, which is a consensus list of the highest priorities for Earth system science that would remove critical barriers impeding progress toward sustainable development. More than 200 scientists and 46 institutions worldwide reviewed the draft of the Grand Challenges. In her notes Denny Taylor wrote:

> In Paris ICSU presented the Grand Challenges for Global Sustainability Research based on the "international consultative process" to:
> - Identify the broadly accepted global sustainability research challenges;
> - Identify high priority research challenges;
> - Mobilize scholars in the physical, social, biological sciences and the humanities to pursue the research that is of critical importance.

The research I am conducting is one response to ICSU's call for participation of scientists across disciplines, paradigms, and professions. As Deliang Chen, the Executive Director of ICSU, stated in Paris at the Open Forum, "The natural sciences should no longer dictate the Earth System research agenda. The social sciences and humanities will be at least as important in its next phase". In the Grand Challenges report the leadership of ICSU to write:

> We know enough to state with a high degree of scientific confidence that without action to mitigate drivers of dangerous global change and enhance societal resilience, humanity has reached a point in history at which changes in climate, hydrological cycles, food systems, sea level, biodiversity, ecosystem services and other factors will undermine development prospects and cause significant human suffering associated with hunger, disease, migration and poverty. If unchecked or unmitigated, these changes will retard or reverse progress towards broadly shared economic, social, environmental and developmental goals.
>
> This is not to say that we do not have sufficient information to act. Our existing knowledge provides a firm basis for vital actions needed to mitigate and adapt to global change. But although we can make progress based on today's knowledge, we will need far more information and understanding to truly solve the problem that global environmental change poses for our societies (p.5).

The Grand Challenges identified by ICSU are:

- *Forecasting*: Improve the usefulness of forecasts of future environmental conditions and their consequences for people;
- *Observations*: Develop the observation systems needed to manage global and regional environmental change;
- *Thresholds*: Determine how to anticipate, recognize, avoid and adapt to abrupt global environmental change;
- *Responses*: Determine what institutional, economic and behavioral changes can enable effective steps toward global sustainability;
- *Innovation*: Encourage innovation (coupled with sound mechanisms for evaluation) in developing technological, policy, and social responses to achieve global sustainability.

The Challenges are not prioritized by ICSU. They are presented as an "indivisible package". ICSU states:

> The concentric circles represent the disciplinary research needed in the social, natural, health and engineering sciences and the humanities that must be carried out alongside interdisciplinary and transdisciplinary research in order to address the challenges. The lines linking the grand challenges show that progress in addressing any challenge will require progress in addressing each of the others (p. 9).

For Denny Taylor the ICSU/ISSC approach reflected her own individual efforts to cross disciplines, paradigms and fields but she wrote papers about her doubts whether the scientists and scholars with whom she often interacted would be able to undertake the border crossings, firstly because their frames of reference were so deeply embedded within their own disciplines and paradigms, and secondly because of the enormous amount of theoretical work that such transdisciplinary perspectives entailed.

The ICSU Grand Challenges Are an Indivisible Package

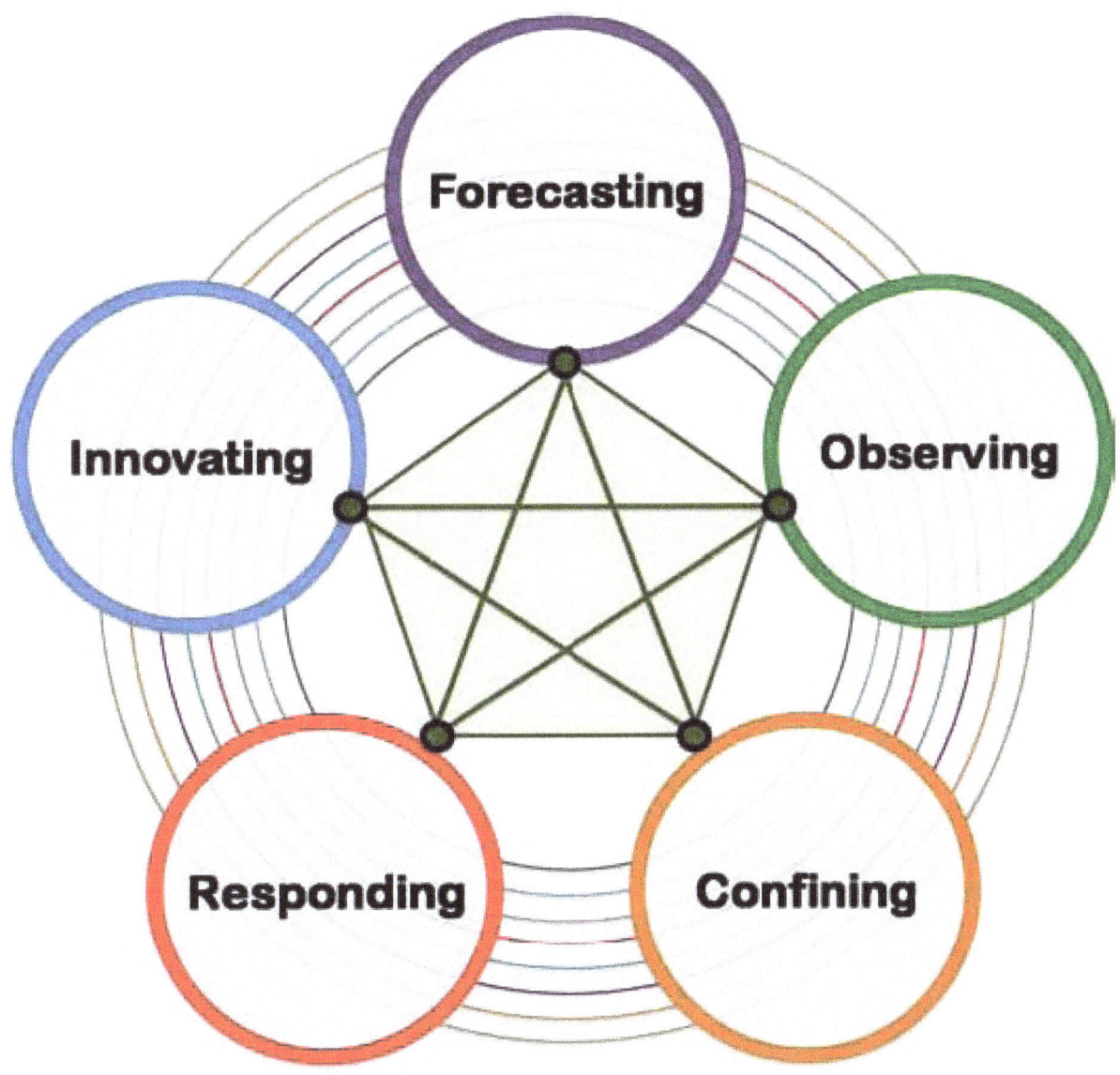

The Grand Challenges identified by ICSU. The Challenges are not prioritized by ICSU, but are presented as an "indivisible package"
PEOPLE AND THE PLANET.

Non-Linear Interrelationships Between Atmospheric and Ecosystem Stressors and Human Activity.

NINETEEN CLUES
GREAT TRANSFORMATIONS CAN BE ACHIEVED THROUGH COLLECTIVE ACTION
GARN PRESS (2014)

A year of intensive research and writing followed, which resulted in four transdisciplinary research papers combining data from the social & physical sciences, qualitative and quantitative, that consciously employed ways of thinking derived from the humanities, especially from works on the philosophy of science. Denny Taylor submitted four proposals based on these papers for the *Planet Under Pressure Global Conference on Earth System Science* that was to take place in London in 2012. All four proposals were peer reviewed and accepted. They focused on: 1) The State of the Planet; 2) Meeting Global Needs; 3) Transforming our way of living; and 4) Governing Across Scales. The abstracts of two papers are included here.

The first paper is entitled: "When the temperature rises more than 2° C what *will* we do? Non linear interrelationships between atmospheric and ecosystem stressors and human activity." The abstract follows:

> When the temperature rises more than 2°C what will we do? What can we learn from our response to present catastrophes, which are increasingly caused by extreme weather conditions associated with climate change? Our present emergency procedures for coping with human and ecological catastrophes are inadequate or non-existent. Given the ever-increasing volume of disasters that people experience worldwide, we should be better prepared. Knowing that the temperature could rise 4°C should galvanize us to support and participate in the planning and preparations.
>
> This paper draws on the findings of ongoing research, which includes emergency first response initiatives and transdisciplinary research on biophysical and social disasters. The research explores "in situ" the impact of the super-complexity of the interconnections between: 1) climate change and extreme weather events; 2) ecological crises; 3) economic crises; 4) extreme wealth; 5) extreme poverty; 6) armed conflict; and 7) public health emergencies. The research considers complementary and contradictory paradigms and metatheories, which are philosophically grounded in different views of science with different histories and traditions. The work re-examines the interconnections between the social, cultural, psychological, biological, and physical sciences, *and* the humanities – philosophy and literature – so that new questions can be asked, new understandings gained, and actions taken.
>
> The non-linear interrelationships between atmospheric and ecosystem stressors and human activity bring into sharp focus the super-complexity of the relationships between the physical, biological and social sciences. The potential for a step change challenges our understandings of the status quo, encourages us to rethink our positionalities within institutions and our relationships with other scientists. Any response to catastrophic events both in the present and in the future will be highly de-

NINETEEN CLUES
GREAT TRANSFORMATIONS CAN BE ACHIEVED THROUGH COLLECTIVE ACTION
GARN PRESS (2014)

pendent on the ability of all those who participate to take into consideration the professional challenges of working with participants who hold different views of science and humanity.

The second paper is entitled: "Unpackaging Human Enterprise and Communicating with the Public" The abstract follows:

In May, 2011, the National Research Council of the US National Academies published the final summary of the four reports entitled *America's Climate Choices* (ACC), noting that while climate change is an international concern, ACC focuses on an "effective *national* response". The following statement frames the report: "Climate change is occurring, is very likely caused by human activities, and poses significant risks for a broad range of human and natural systems. … In the judgment of the Committee on America's Climate Choices, the environmental, economic, and humanitarian risks of climate change indicate *a pressing need for substantial action* to limit the magnitude of climate change and to prepare to adapt to its impacts". In this presentation I will argue that if we wait for a response from global leaders and policy makers it might be too late.

If the US Congress has been presented with this information, and if governments around the world are aware of the dire circumstances in which we find ourselves, why are they doing so little about it?

The *unpackaging of human enterprise* and the *re-earthing of people* will take the efforts of scientists and scholars in the humanities working together to expose the negative consequences of the protection of invested interests by governments, which in turn are compromised by the aggressive competition of geopolitical markets and the greed of the global financial institutions, which provide the tipping elements for a step change for the planet and humanity. In the spirit of Stephen Toulmin, it is going to take millions of people, of widely differing and disconnected values, ethics, emotions, spiritual beliefs, levels of trust, interest and power, working together in small groups and organizations to ensure that billions of people do not lose their lives in the struggle to survive.

Convinced by her research on Earth systems and the geopolitical to the increasing existential risks to children, families, and communities on local, national and global scales, Denny Taylor produced a document which she entitled: *Nineteen Clues: Great Transformations Can Be Achieved Through Collective Action*, which was subsequently published by Garn Press. This text addressed the question first posed by ICSU/ISSC in the Grand Challenges document, which Denny Taylor called "the question of questions", which she referred to as the "QoQ":

How can timely actions be undertaken at unprecedented and multiple geopolitical scales, when the issues involve people of widely differing—and—disconnected values, ethics, emotions, spiritual beliefs, levels of trust, interests and power?

Written prior to concerns about "fake news" and "alternate facts", in *Nineteen Clues* she encourages readers to go to the primary sources on climate change and other existential phenomena, and using *The New York Times* as a point of entry she demonstrates the strategies the public can use to access primary sources of scientific information. Here are the nineteen clues to solving the QoQ:

- **FIRST CLUE**: People are changing the planet and the planet is changing people.

- **SECOND CLUE**: The first step to American participation in saving the world is the recognition of the legitimacy of global concerns about US overconsumption of the Earth's finite resources, and the negative impact it is having on the planet and its people.

- **THIRD CLUE**: Extreme social inequality in the US negatively impacts American society, increases the pressures on the planet, and has a cascading adverse effect on global stability and sustainability.

- **FOURTH CLUE**: In the US further economic growth will not improve the health or well-being of the American people. Greater emphasis on income equality and less emphasis on economic growth will diminish US over-exploitation of planet's irreplaceable resources.

- **FIFTH CLUE**: Inequality in America is bad for the planet as well as for people, and increases our ethical responsibility to act.

- **SIXTH CLUE**: While poor women and children in the US are the most disadvantaged, all American women and children are disadvantaged when compared with women and children in other developed countries.

- **SEVENTH CLUE**: The planet cannot be protected unless the rights of women and children are protected.

- **EIGHTH CLUE**: In the US the war on climate science and on the health and wellbeing of women and children is a symptom of a pathological political ideology that negatively impacts global stability and sustainability of life on the planet.

- **NINTH CLUE**: In the US the cascading effects of powerbrokers' maladaptive decision making is quite literally changing the geology of the planet, the chemistry of the air we breathe, and the water we drink.

- **TENTH CLUE**: Global action to avoid social or planetary tipping points will need to include the active participation of the US in rethinking K-12 education to make schools more equitable and just, and to reconnect children with the natural world.

- **ELEVENTH CLUE**: In teaching the young we teach ourselves, and we will come to understand that the Earth is not an infinite resource to be exploited, but a finite life force that we must care for and sustain.

- **TWELFTH CLUE**: One in four American children lives in poverty, nearly 60 percent more than in 1974, and the number of people living in severe poverty has reached a record high. A national study in 2009 found that one in fifty children in America is homeless and living in a shelter, motel, car, shared housing, abandoned building, park or orphanage. The proportions in some school districts exceed one in ten, and the number is growing rapidly.

- **THIRTEENTH CLUE**: The ideological doctrine of the American Legislative Exchange Council (ALEC) makes it easy to understand how the great wealth and vast power of the private sector is undermining not only the US -12 public school system, but is also undermining the US response to climate change.

- **FOURTEENTH CLUE**: Equitable public education should be an inalienable right of every child that policy makers must protect. It is their responsibility not to sell children to private corporations that force children to become captive consumers of products that damage their minds and increase their levels of anxiety.

- **FIFTEENTH CLUE**: The problem is that no one in Washington is listening.

- **SIXTEENTH CLUE**: At no time in the future will US political, corporate or financial decision makers, Democrats, Republicans, or Plutocrats, be able to deny knowledge of the anthropogenic changes that are taking place, or to cover up the fact that for power, privilege, and profit they did nothing about it.

- **SEVENTEENTH CLUE**: There are signs of hope within US society. There are many groups of people working together and acting as our guides in re-Earthing. One site of resistance is K-12 schools. Even though the pressures are great, teachers, principals and parents are organizing, establishing websites, arranging meetings, holding rallies, signing petitions, opting out of testing, and sending unopened boxes of tests back to Pearson.

- **EIGHTEENTH CLUE**: The key components in the struggle for social and environmental sustainability identified by the delegates at the Planet Under Pressure global conversation were: (1) the active engagement of people; (2) the participation of diverse social groups working together; (3) a focus on human well being; (4) the development of political will; and (5) ethical and principled global agreements.

- **NINETEENTH CLUE**: The brute power of ideology and great wealth is used to distort and discredit science, but it cannot change the scientific evidence and is no match for the courage and endurance of scientists who stand their ground or for the people who support them.

PHOTO
Climate Change March,
New York City, 2014

Student Teachers as First Responders in the Aftermath of Hurricane Sandy.

EVERY STUDENT TEACHER BECAME A FIRST RESPONDER IN THE AFTERMATH OF THE STORM
THEIR LIVED EXPERIENCE OF THIS CATASTROPHIC EVENT BECAME
A VITAL PART OF THE COURSE

By 2012 Denny Taylor was engaged in research on the risks of the transgression of planetary boundaries and the cataclysmic consequences for all humankind. Years of ethnographic research with families and children in vulnerable communities convinced her that the corporate transmission of workforce skills in K-12 public schools was/is having cascading effects on U.S. society, endangering children and future generations by rapidly accelerating ways of life on the planet that are unsustainable. In the fall semester of 2012 she was teaching the masters and doctoral course "Family, Community, and School Literacies: Cultural Perspectives" when Hurricane Sandy devastated the Long Island communities in which her students were teaching.

Every student in her class became a first responder in the aftermath of the storm, and their family and school experiences in in the schools and communities where they lived and worked became a vital part of the course. In her notes Denny Taylor wrote:

> The dynamic complexity of the interrelationships between the various research assignments and the deep scholarship required of their family literacy book study groups were well represented on the long rolls of paper on which they created their audit trails. At the beginning of December the students were still resolved to keep the course tradition of a family literacy celebration on the last night of class,

PHOTO
Aftermath of Hurricane Sandy, 2012

and as the end of the semester approached the presentation of their research and projects took on added significance as they prepared for the event. Mothers and fathers, sisters and brothers, partners and friends were invited, and students spoke amongst themselves before and after class about the complicated logistics of family members getting off work, traveling in the rush hour, and finding parking.

I had ordered pizza that night as I did most weeks, and the students worked intensely, checking the time to make sure all their work would be complete, some of them laughing and chatting, volunteering to take projects home to finish as they prepared for the family literacy night the following week. Much of their attention was taken with the completion of their massive group audit trails tracing their progress through the course, which would be on the walls as graphic representations of the embedded complexity of literacy practices in family, community, and schools settings that had been the focus of their research and readings.

Then added to the research projects that were on the syllabus they decided to add one of their own and they included it on the agenda. Working across groups they developed a new family literacy survey on the uses of digital literacies, which would be the "Ice Breaker" at the celebration. Also on the agenda was "Family and Community Response to Hurricane Sandy", which would be a student led conversation about the ways in which the literacies of the hurricane had infused so many of their projects and activities.

At the end of class I reminded everyone that my hope was that by organizing a family literacy night for our class they would organize similar family literacy nights in their schools for their students and their families. I encouraged them to take the lead the following week, but agreed to make a PowerPoint presentation at the end of the celebration that would include photos I had taken throughout the semester as students worked on their audit trails and made their book study group presentation. The class left noisily, gathering up materials for projects that were not quite finished, checking with each other about last minute arrangements about the food they planned to bring. Then came the second disaster.

Student Teachers Respond to the Sandy Hook Mass Killing of Twenty Kindergarten and First Grade Children and Six Educators.

THE FAMILY LITERACY NIGHT PLANNED BEFORE SANDY HOOK
BECAME A VITAL ASPECT OF THE WORK THE STUDENTS DID TO COPE WITH THE MASSACRE
AND PREPARE FOR EVENTS IN SCHOOLS THAT THEY MIGHT THEMSELVES EXPERIENCE

Two days after the preparations for the Family Literacy Celebration in which her graduate students were to reflect on their first response efforts during Hurricane Sandy, the mass shooting and death of 20 kindergarten and first grade children and six educators at the Sandy Hook Elementary School in Newtown Connecticut took place. In her notes Denny Taylor wrote:

> The Sandy Hook Elementary School mass shooting of twenty kindergarten and first grade children and their principal, school psychologist and teachers took place that Friday, December 14, 2012, creating a moment so profoundly incomprehensible and painful it was as if life stopped.

On December 19, 2012, five days after the Sandy Hook Massacre Denny Taylor drove to Newtown with Josefa Pace, one of her doctoral students whose doctoral dissertation focused on the lives and literacies of four immigrant women and their families who left Italy in the 1930's and made their homes in New York, Arizona, and Argentina. Quietly and unobtrusively they photographed the prayers, poems, cards of condolence, drawings, and notes – any text which contained words, symbols, or pictorial images – and then they moved on to photograph the flowers, balloons, teddy bears and toys people had left in memoriam of the 20 kindergarten children and six educators. Their task was to make sure that during a few hours on this one-day every message was carefully photographed and preserved before being gathered and processed into sacred soil for a permanent memorial in Newtown. For Denny Taylor these photos would become a data set that she would spend months analyzing, but her immediate task was to prepare for the family literacy event she had planned with her masters and doctoral students. Here is her account of that event:

> It was Monday by the time I could think about the class and the family literacy celebration. I thought back to the class the day after the destruction of the Twin Towers, but this time it was more complicated, if that is possible, since students were bringing their friends and families for a celebration.
>
> Digging deep after the Newtown tragedy when we met for class and what was going to be a family literacy celebration, as I had done after September 11, 2001, I asked the graduate students if they wanted to cancel class, if

they wanted to talk about the mass killing, how they would like to proceed. No one wanted to cancel but no one wanted to talk either. Students shook their heads, some closing their eyes others with their hands over their mouths. Some were in tears, and as I looked around the room, for a minute or two I was also holding back tears. Looking around the room I could not help thinking that these young teachers, just beginning their careers, were the same age as the young teachers who were killed in the mass shooting at the Sandy Hook Elementary School.

I don't remember what I said to them at that moment. I know I spoke about the courage of teachers, of the principal and teachers who had died in their attempts to protect the children and of the courage of the teachers who had survived. I told them that in the aftermath of every catastrophic event I have known, it was teachers, often very young women, who took care of the children, comforted the families, and organized the relief effort in their schools and communities. I encouraged them to make sure they kept the documents I had given them on teachers as first responders in their desks in their classrooms and to share them with other teachers.

One student had brought her mother and another student her mother and father. One had brought her two sisters and her brother who was away at college but had come home so he could come to class with his sister for the celebration. Others too, had come, partners, friends, but no young children were there that night. Perhaps it was just as well. In my welcome I said I had taken it upon myself to reorganize the evening, and that the presentation I had intended to give at the end of the evening I was now going to give at the beginning. However, it would be less of a presentation and more of a dedication, a eulogy, a remembrance, with some thoughts about how we learn to go on. I had taken a photo from the New York Times of the signpost for Sandy Hook Elementary School and I used it at the beginning of the PowerPoint. We stood for two minutes of silence and then I read from the screen.

"What happened at Sandy Hook Elementary School is the tragedy of all tragedies, but as Robbie Parker, whose 6 year old daughter, Emily, is among the dead, said: "as we move on from what happened here and what happened to so many people, let us not let it turn into something that defines us".

"Robbie Parker's words were taken up by President Obama when he said, "As a community, you've inspired us, Newtown. In the face of indescribable violence, in the face of unconscionable evil, you've looked out for each other, and you've cared for one another, and you've loved one another. This is how Newtown will be remembered".

"To foster resiliency in children," I continued to read, "it is important that we do everything we can to create schools as safe, joyful, playful places *before* catastrophic events take place. *If* children are to have the maximum opportunity to recover from potentially traumatizing experiences. Every effort should be made to:

- Establish schools as safe, joyful places for children and teachers;
- Ensure that schools are nurturing and fun environments in which play is central to the curriculum;
- Recognize the importance of the languages children speak and respect their heritage and national identity;
- Promote children's health and well being by

PHOTO
Five days after the Sandy Hook Massacre, people came to Newtown and left toys letters, poems, prayers, photos, teddy bears and the lion with a message for Jessie who was killed in the mass shooting.

- providing them with opportunities to sing, dance and play musical instruments;
- Enhance academic learning through literacy activities, art and science projects, and other meaning making practices;
- Welcome families and encourage parents and caregivers to actively participate in the life of the school through events that incorporate music, theater, dance, science, and literature.

On the next slide was a quote from Maxine Greene from her book, *Releasing the Imagination*:

> Our classrooms ought to be nurturing and thoughtful and just all at once they ought to pulsate with multiple conceptions of what it is to be human and alive.

It was enough. In death the possibility for the reaffirmation of life rebounds. On that night, as we all thought of the children and teachers who had been shot and killed, it was the lives of the young graduate students who had become teachers and the lives of the children that they would teach that we were there to celebrate. The slides that followed included photos of the students working on their literacy projects. In addition to the photos of them working in class on their audit trails. I had incorporated photos of their finished projects which they had given me. Hurricane Sandy and the literacies that were the signature of the storm were also represented.

At the end I included a photo of a child who had traveled from Australia with her mother who planned to run in the New York City Marathon. When the event was cancelled because of the storm, many runners ran anyway to raise funds for families whose homes and neighborhoods were badly damaged by the storm. The little girl had made a sign to cheer on the runners, and she held it up high as her mother passed by. I used the photo to cheer on my students and to let them know how proud I was of them for their courage and endurance in a time that does not look kindly on either teachers or children.

The students picked up where I left off with the digital literacies survey that they had constructed, getting out their cell phones and working with family and friends to respond to the questions. Pens in hand they wrote down responses in the old fashioned way. There were serious conversations, laughter, friendly disagreements, and a few tutorials that took place as they worked together. The questions included: What forms of social media do you use?; How do you access these forms of social media?; What types of electronics/technology are you currently carrying with you?;Do you read digital texts? (e.g. eBooks?); How do you access current news? (e.g. newspapers, computer, television, etc.); Do you shop on-line or in-person?; At what age do you believe it is appropriate to get a cell phone?; Do you like to write with a pen, a pencil, or a computer?;Do you prefer paper receipts or e-receipts?; Do you text? If so, approximately how many times do you text a day?; Approximately how many hours do you spend in front of the television and/or computer each day?; Do you prefer to send a letter or an email?; Do you speak or write in another language? If so, how does your language use influence you use of electronic media?; Do you write music, plays, poems, or stories? If so do you use electronic sources in composing and writing?; Do you use electronic navigational aps? If so when was the last time you used a map instead of MapQuest or a GPS?; How do you use digital literacies to communicate with your family and friends?

The pizza was long gone and the food students had brought was quickly disappearing when we brought the questions of digital literacies back to the whole group. Students used the "findings" of their digital literacy surveys to introduce their guests. When the introductions and surveys were done the father of one of the students asked how many texts everyone sent and received in a day. The boyfriend of one of the students said, "450". "That's about right," the younger brother of another student, who was an undergraduate at an upstate university and had come home especially. There were exclamations from some of the students and disbelief from several older family members in the room, and that's all it took for energetic discussions to take place about the digital gap.

The evening ended with students talking with their guests about the journey they had taken in the construction of their audit trails, which pulled all their projects and readings together and incorporated the metaphors they had created for the literacies that they discovered, which are integral to ways we live our lives in families, communities, and schools. There were last class goodbyes, and as everyone left one student lingered for a moment to thank me for what I had said at the beginning of class. "I didn't want to come to class tonight," she told me. She said it was as if her life just stopped when she heard "what happened". She added, "I'm glad I came".

It was the last class in the last course that Denny Taylor taught at Hofstra. In the spring of 2013 she was on sabbatical and then retired and was awarded emeritus status. By this time she was convinced that human societies had reached a tipping point and that we were walking a line between survival of the human species and mass extinction. The existential risks were increasing exponentially, but were largely being ignored by the political powers who could make a difference. In one of her notebooks she wrote:

- If we do not support scientists there will be no planet for our children to inhabit;
- If we do not support public school teachers our children will not be prepared for the perils they will face both now and in the future;
- If we do not support the lives of everybody's child there will be no children alive on Earth;
- Our children will become endlings in the full sense of the word.

The Deception: Protecting Assault Weapons Is More Important than Protecting Children's Lives

THE CHILDREN OF SANDY HOOK VS. THE U.S. CONGRESS AND GUN VIOLENCE IN AMERICA

AN ANALYSIS OF THE CONGRESSIONAL HEARINGS AND SUBCOMMITTEE MEETINGS ON THE 2013 ASSAULT WEAPONS BAN BILL

DENNY TAYLOR

"This book is timely and engaging. I was blown away by the detail and the reasoned argument amidst the horror." – Yohuru Williams

The Founding of Garn Press to Support Writers of Conscience Providing Vital Information to the Public on the Perils Facing People and the Planet.

GARN PRESS PUBLISHING
WWW.GARNPRESS.COM | WWW.FACEBOOK.COM/GARNPRESS

The QoQ remained uppermost in her mind but the desire to make a practical difference in the lives of scientists and teachers became of paramount importance to her. Theory is of no use unless it is attached in some way to the lived world. Knowing that the perils her granddaughter's generation will face are far greater than any perils her generation will face, she sold her house and car moved into a studio apartment in New York City, using some of the money derived from the sale to found Garn Press. David Taylor, her lifelong friend to whom she was once married, and their son, Benjamin Taylor, who had just completed a master's degree at NYU in social policy, became co-founders of the press. It is the synergy between them and their complimentary talents and skills that have enabled them to establish the three divisions at Garn Press that were derived from Denny Taylor's research:

PEOPLE AND THE PLANET: At Garn Press we are energized for social action. We support peaceful social movements that connect people and the planet.

Garn Press is interested in the insights to be gained from the unimagined circumstances in which people find themselves, especially due to climate change and the changing ecology of the planet. We are interested in books that challenge the status quo, that shake us up and make us think about the odd and the anomalous, that are becoming commonplace in our everyday lives.

At a time when there is overwhelming scientific evidence that people and the planet are on an unsustainable course, this small publishing press is gutsy enough to think it might have a small role to play by publishing books that ask how a society that values logic and reason can be so blind to the imminent cascading risks that exist? At Garn Press we question our human fallibility, and we ask why our human instinct for survival has not kicked in?

What concerns us at Garn Press is whether the scientific community can deliver *actionable knowledge* that will provide new insights and solutions to solve real world problems. We worry about *how timely* these *actions* will be if scientists *deliver* actionable knowledge to global leaders, especially the US Congress, but no actions are taken.

PEOPLE AND SOCIETY: At Garn Press we are determined to participate in the peaceful struggle for economic, racial and gender equality, and for the cessation of violence and armed conflict. We take seriously the democratic imperative to challenge the avarice and greed of large global corporations, and the misuse of power by governments.

Garn Press is interested in books that inhabit that uncomfortable space between people and policy makers. Our mission is making knowledge work for social action, and through the global publication of hardcover, paperback and eBooks, Garn Press supports peaceful social movements for human rights and social justice. In this time of grand challenges when our human fabric is being stretched and strained, the public need to have non-technical access to disciplinary research in the social, natural, health and engineering sciences, and it is of considerable importance that interdisciplinary and transdisciplinary research is similarly made available with insights from the humanities encouraging creative solutions to life-threatening problems. If we are to survive, addressing these problems must include deep reflection and lasting conversations on equity ad justice for all.

Garn Press asks, for example, why so many books on people and society that are well reasoned and supported by science are banned and their authors denigrated? Ironically, many of these books focus on the ways in which we educate our children, and the irreparable damage that can be caused by the high stakes tests associated with the Common Core. Garn Press is interested in the circumstances that allow such book banning to occur, and also in the consequences for the public because of their disenfranchisement by the authoritative manipulation of what is written and what is read.

Garn Press is particularly interested in cautionary tales about the obfuscation of information through textual maneuvers that are carefully orchestrated to cover up those slips of the pen that are made to maintain the privilege and power of a few — this especially includes books that uncover the nefarious practices of corporate reformers and the concerted effort that is underway to dismantle public schools and privatize them, not just in the U.S. but worldwide.

IMAGINATION AND THE HUMAN SPIRIT: At Garn Press, we are convinced that actionable knowledge to address some of the great questions about human life depends on nurturing the imagination and human spirit. Through the arts people are inspired to act.

For Garn Press, science, literature, art, and philosophy are not separate categories. They are intricately connected, and through these connections it is possible for us to get a larger sense of life, with a clarity of vision that would not be possible otherwise.

At Garn we are convinced that without art the sciences have the creativity sucked out of them. Most scientists and artists get this, even though most policy makers do not. Similar to Italo Calvino, Garn's stance is that science, literature, philosophy and art create epicenters of creativity, vortexes of energy, and an aesthetic experience, that provides insights science or art alone cannot.

In a recent post on the Garn Press website Denny Taylor wrote:

David Joseph Kolb, the Pulitzer nominated journalist and author of the prize winning Garn Press novel *Devil Knows*, writes:

> Garn Press of New York City is rapidly making its voice heard and appreciated as a bastion of humanism and science in the world. Please support Garn's heroic efforts to restore decency, education and justice to their rightful seats in the societal order.

At Garn we are dedicated to publishing books by writers of conscience and courage. Our books are literary, experimental, and based on well-documented scientific evidence. They are written by renowned scholars, great scientists and teachers, novelists and essayists, and children's authors and illustrators who are determined to make a difference in the world. Garn is publishing both nonfiction and fiction books for adults and children that:

- Recognize the importance of the everyday lives of children, families, and communities and support their participation in the collective struggle for equity and justice for all people;
- Take into consideration that the great acceleration in climate and ecological change when combined with geopolitical uncertainty are increasing existential risks to children, families, communities;
- Support the idea that great transformations can be achieved through collective action at local, national and global scales;
- Provide indisputable research evidence from scientists on climate change and the impact of people on the planet;
- Value diversity and the struggle for racial, economic, social and gender justice;
- Seize the moment to explore the political awakening of young people and their role as cultural change makers;
- Support parents and teachers resisting the assault on U.S. public schools by right wing politicians and corporate education reformers;
- Share the courageous stories of families as they support loved ones who are vulnerable or terminally ill;
- Imagine the possibilities of peacemaking to counter problems of bullying in schools and in society;
- Take us into uncharted territory of new forms of storytelling that excite, delight, and sometimes exasperate:
- Make us laugh, are joyful, and encourage us to have fun!

Denny Taylor was the editor working directly with authors on the following books. First, here are the works of fiction:

- *You're Not Dead* (2016, 2017 new edition), Geoff Ward, Principal of Homerton College and Deputy Vice-Chancellor, University of Cambridge, Chairman of the Fitzwilliam Museum Syndicate;
- *Blowing Out The Candles* (2013, 2015), James Paul Gee, Mary Lou Fulton Presidential Professor at Arizona State University;
- *Black Inked Pearl: A Girl's Quest* (2015), Ruth Finnegan, Emeritus Professor, The Open University, Fellow of the British Academy, Honorary Fellow of Somerville College Oxford;
- *Flush: The Exaggerated Memoir of a Fourth Grade Scaredy-Cat Super-Hero* (2016), Rick Meyer, Professor and chair of the Department of Language, Literacy, & Sociocultural Studies, University of New Mexico;
- *Devil Knows* (2015): A Tale of Murder and Madness in America's First Century (2015), David Joseph Kolb;
- *The Smart One* (2015), Ken Goodman, Professor Emeritus, Language Reading and Culture, at the University of Arizona;
- *Bloody Lane* (2015), Martin E. Lee, full-time freelance ed-

ucational writer; and Matthew C. Fleury, freelance writer in English language arts educational publishing.

Here are the non-fiction books:

- *The Educator And The Oligarch* (2014, 2016), Anthony Cody, co-founder of the Network for Public Education, National Board certified teacher;
- *What's Whole in Whole Language in the 21st Century?* (2014), Ken Goodman, Professor Emeritus, Language, Reading, and Culture, College of Education, University of Arizona;
- *Beware the Roadbuilders: Literature as Resistance* (2015), P.L. Thomas, Professor of Education, Furman University, Greenville, SC;
- *Raising Peacemakers* (2015), Esther Sokolov Fine, Professor Emerita of Education, York University, Toronto, Canada;
- *Preparing the Nation's Teachers to Teach Reading: A Manifesto in Defense of "Teacher Educators Like Me"*, (2015), Curt Dudley-Marling;
- *A Parent's Guide to Public Education in the 21st Century: Navigating Education Reform to Get the Best Education for My Child* (2016), Russ Walsh, Public School Teacher and College Instructor;
- *5-13: A Memoir of Love, Loss and Survival* (2016), Nancy Rankie Shelton, Professor of Education at UMBC in Baltimore, Maryland;
- *Negotiating a Permeable Curriculum: On Literacy, Diversity, and the Interplay of Children's and Teachers' Worlds* (2016), Anne Haas Dyson, Faculty Excellence Professor, College of Education, University of Illinois at Urbana-Champaign; and Bobbie Kabuto, Associate Professor of Literacy Education in the Elementary and Early Childhood Education Department, Queens College, City University of New York;
- *First, Do No Harm: Progressive Education in a Time of Existential Risk* (2016), Steve Nelson, Head of Calhoun School, NYC, 1998-2017;
- *Every Least Sparrow* (2017), Carolyn H. Walker, journalist and creative writing instructor;
- *Trumplandia: Unmasking Post-Truth America* (2017), P.L. Thomas, Professor of Education, Furman University, Greenville, SC;
- *United We Stand Divided We Fall: Resisting Trump's Agenda: Essays On Protest And Resistance And What We Can Do To Stop Him* (2017); George Lakoff, Emeritus Professor of Cognitive Science and Linguistics at the University of California at Berkeley; Jonathan Foley, Executive Director of the California Academy of Sciences; Yohuru R. Williams, Professor and Dean of the College of Arts and Sciences at the University of St. Thomas, Minnesota; and 14 other authors;
- *Playhouse: Optimistic Stories of Real Hope for Families with Little Children* (2017), Monica Taylor, Professor and Deputy Chair of the Department of Secondary and Special Education at Montclair State University;
- *The Gadfly on the Wall: A Public School Teacher Speaks Out on Racism and Reform* (2017), Steven Singer, National Board Certified Language Arts teacher, Director of the Research and Blogging Committee for the Badass Teachers Association, and co-founder of the Pennsylvania-based education budget advocacy group T.E.A.C.H.

In addition to these books that Garn Press has published in the past three years Garn has also published two YA novels, two children's books, and four non-fiction books that Denny Taylor has written, plus two non-fiction books that she has edited. All of these books are fictional reiterations of positions she has taken in her research on families, language, literacy and trauma, and on climate and ecological change and existential risk.

Young Adult Novels:

- *Rosie's Umbrella* (2014, 2017) (psychological mystery, and coal-mining family literacy and immigrant story. An eighth grade girl's political awakening);
- *Split Second Solution* (2016) (dystopian fantasy set in NYC in which the central character is a 22-year-old young woman who is French-North African. Reflects the findings of forty years of novel and eerily parallels events taking place and foretells what quite possibly could happen in 2022).

Children's Picture Story Books:

- *Toodle-oo Ruby Blue!* (2017) (It's hard to say goodbye at any age but especially when you are young. This is a playful fantasy about two little girls finding it hard to say "goodbye" after playing together);
- *Rat-a-tat-tat! I've Lost My Cat!* (2015) (Losing someone or something is as hard as saying goodbye. A little girl solves a mystery when her aunt is upset because she has lost her cat).

Non-fiction:

- *Nineteen Clues: Great Transformations Can Be Achieved Through Collective Action* (2013, 2014) (Based on transdisciplinary research across the social and physical sciences and scholarship in the humanities. A book for the public encouraging social and political action in response to climate change and the dismantling of public education);
- *The Children of Sandy Hook vs. The U.S. Congress and Gun Violence in America* (2017) (Based on the photographic record created 5 days after the mass shooting and a document analysis of the Congressional committee hearings on the 2013 Assault Weapon Ban bill);
- *United We Stand Divided We Fall: Resisting Trump's Agenda: Essays On Protest And Resistance And What We Can Do To Stop Him* (with 16 other authors – writers of conscience and world renowned scholars, 2017);
- *Teaching without Testing: Assessing the Complexity of Children's Literacy Learning* (2017) (Based on the Biographic Literacy Profiles Project – BliPP – which took place in the 1980's, with an introduction by Bobbie Kabuto);
- *Save Our Children, Save Our School, Pearson Broke the Golden Rule* (2014) (A political satire using actual statements made by nine very powerful men and twelve venerable women scholars. Macbeth, Noam Chomsky, and Louis C.K. all appear and participate in this romp about climate change, extreme wealth, and public education);
- *Romance of Mathematics* (2015) (A nineteenth century satire on mathematics and gender with a introduction by Denny Taylor).

Reflecting on the first three years of Garn Press in the 2016-2017 Winter Catalogue, Denny Taylor wrote:

Three years ago Garn did not exist. Now we are publishing award-winning nonfiction that explores compelling ideas and arguments based on primary research and investigative reporting ignored by mainstream media. We're actively supporting writers of conscience who offer original research-based perspectives on the most pressing issues of our day including: climate change, inequality, privatization of public education, children with special needs, armed conflict; gun violence, death and dying, cancer (love, loss, and survival), and many other critical factors jeopardizing social, economic, and environmental sustainability.

In addition to books Garn Press is publishing articles and commentaries by many renowned educators, artists, and scientists. But at Garn we do not consider this enough. We're also committed to nurturing the imagination and human spirit by publishing great novels and poetry. Garn's award winning novelists and poets share this ideal, and all the fiction books published by Garn – whether mysteries, fantasies, or historical novels – are written not only to entertain, but also to raise serious questions about time, memory and whether what we see – in life as well as in the mirror – is what is really what is occurring.

That three people – Ben, David and I – with the good will of authors, and with our many readers cheering us on, have been able to produce all this gives you some idea how serious we take the debt we owe our children for what we have done to the planet and to the society we are handing to them.

There's much more, of course. The Garn Press website that Ben has created is groundbreaking in the publishing industry, with few parallels. It is visually appealing and content-rich and we publish new and original content on a daily basis, not only about Garn authors and books, but also articles, editorials, and commentaries. We're conducting author interviews and producing videos, audios, print interviews and readings by every author, and posting them on the Garn Press website. And, we're featuring World News Commentary – editorials and articles that are not filtered as they are in the mainstream media, which include posts based on communications with many scientists and thought leaders here in the U.S., including Noam Chomsky, George Lakoff, and many scientists around the world, including the glaciologist Jason Box who is engaged in some of the most prescient research and commentary in the social and physical sciences.

SPLIT SECOND SOLUTION
GARN PRESS (2016)

Conclusion: The Struggle in the Public Arena to Make Earth A Child Safe Zone.

SAVE OUR CHILDREN, SAVE OUR SCHOOL, PEARSON BROKE THE GOLDEN RULE
GARN PRESS (2015)

Denny Taylor continues to work with writers of conscience, mentoring them as she did her doctoral students. She is an editor to illustrious scholars at the Universities of Cambridge and Oxford, as well as being a brave, empathetic and sometime formidable researcher in her own right. In the following passage from her two TEDx talks posted on the Garn Press website, she reflects on her lifetime of research and fieldwork including her own life experience. In *Can Books Change the World?* She writes:

> Based on the evidence of science we know that an unbelievable step change has taken place, and there has been a massive shift in our thinking about climate change because of all the information that is available through social media links to the primary sources of data on what is happening to people and the planet.
>
> It is now a well-accepted scientific fact that we have left the 10,000 years of stable weather patterns that were the signature of our beloved Holocene, and we have entered the Anthropocene which is hotter, wetter, drier, more turbulent, unpredictable and polluted because of human activity.
>
> In my mind I can reach back and hold the hands of my grandmothers who were born in the 19th century in a coal-mining villages in Wales. Still further back, I have been held in the arms of my paternal great grandmother who was born in the 1860's.
>
> And I can reach forward with my other hand and quite literally hold the hand of my granddaughter, who was born at the beginning of the 21st century, who I held in my arms when she was a baby and is now preparing to go to college.
>
> But it is not just that my life spans three centuries, or that I was born in a different millennium than my granddaughter. What is totally astounding to me is that I was born in a different Epoch to her and to the millennials who mean so much to me.
>
> Boomers – my generation – were born in the epoch of the Holocene, while the children of Boomers, and certainly Millennials, are the first generation of the Anthropocene.
>
> If you are of my generation your grandchildren will never experience life on the planet before climate change. They will never experience the time when we were absolutely sure that doomsday is billions of years away. They know that it is not, and many that I know are afraid that they will become endlings – the last people to live on Earth.
>
> My generation, born in the last century of the Holocene, is bequeathing to young people lives that are anthropogenic in a new century, a new millennium and a new epoch that brings with it less certainty and many challenges that we ourselves have not had to face. ...
>
> We who live small lives cannot solve the vast problem of climate change, but we can contribute to the struggle.
>
> We know in our hearts and in our minds that there is one fact that is indisputable: *If* human societies are to survive in the long term as well as the short term, it is imperative we do everything we can to increase the resilience of the social systems that are the foundation of our democratic life.
>
> It is absolutely critical that we all work together to maintain cohesion within society and that we support the care-giving professionals who work in the social institutions that are essential if human societies are going to survive.
>
> We are not backwards in coming forwards in stating that we do *not* consider the oligarchs who use their money in divisive ways to dictate social policy, to be of any importance to us now.
>
> We reject the political action committees – the PAC's – that are jeopardizing our democracy and delaying the government's response to the greatest disaster humanity has ever faced.
>
> We know rich men will not save us.
>
> If we are to survive it will be because teachers and nurses of conscience, and all those in the other caring professions who are at the center of our society, make it pos-

SAVE OUR CHILDREN, SAVE OUR SCHOOL, PEARSON BROKE THE GOLDEN RULE
GARN PRESS (2015)

sible for our children not only to survive but thrive.

And, in the TEDx talk, *What About the Kids? Tackling Climate Change for Our Children*, she writes:

> The enduring message is that children need their families, schools, and communities to be safe joyful places *before* disasters occur if they are going to have the opportunity to recover when disasters occur.
>
> In the years to come, as anthropogenic change intensifies and catastrophic events occur more frequently, as will undoubtedly happen, it is parents who will rise to the challenge to protect their children, and teachers who will invariably be first responders when disasters do occur.
>
> We might not have faith in governments, but we do have faith in people, in the ability for parents and teachers to quickly morph from the ordinary to the extraordinary, to take a leadership role *and to act*, when our "leaders" are bogged down in the increased polarization of the political process and are too burdened by their privilege and money to act.
>
> Power brokers will do well to remember that we are not just appealing to their humanity, which has been found sadly lacking. Our appeal is based on science, on empirical research on human development, on research on language and learning, on anthropological research, on sociological, psychological, medical and psychiatric research, and now, in recent decades, on research in Earth system science, all of which have brought into sharp focus the indivisible relationships between people and the planet.
>
> If our children are to survive and thrive in this century, it is imperative that we prepare them with new forms of "worldliness". In their backpacks and tool-kits the "worldliness" they will need is a perspective on life which values imagination, creativity, originality, and innovation, one that is deeply rooted in Earth-human history, is grounded in the present time of human dissonance with the planet and does not flinch from addressing human conflicts that we experience with each other. In tackling climate change for our children it is imperative that we are vigilant and sensitive to the limited time that they will have to find new ways to sustain human life *on* the planet and to live more closely *with* Earth.

Denny Taylor encourages all of us to be brave, be fearless and not forget. With many others she is convinced that we must imagine the extraordinary opportunities we have to respond to the anthropogenic changes taking place here on Earth. She is a humanistic thinker of humble origins who lives humbly in these most challenging of times. Her family literacy research created a portal through which she has helped us see the systemic complexity of the relationships between people and the planet. She is also convinced that unless we act soon, the great acceleration in human transgression of the planetary boundaries will, in a very short period of time, have a catastrophic impact on everybody's child, but especially on children who live in deep poverty both in the U.S. and around the world who are already suffering the consequences of climate change. And yet she is hopeful, putting her trust in people to organize and make it known that we are willing to risk everything, even our own lives, to make the planet a child safe zone.

Addendum.

Transdisciplinary Research Graphics Making the Planet a Child Safe Zone.

THESE TRANSDISCIPLINARY GRAPHICS REJECT CARTESIAN WAYS OF THINKING
THEY ARE DYNAMIC IN COMPLEXITY, SYSTEMIC IN ORIENTATION, AND ALL EVENTS ARE CONTINGENT AND CONDITIONAL

Denny Taylor has used graphics, such as the ones here, throughout her life as a researcher. The systemic complexity of every node on every graphic represents months and sometimes years of fieldwork and analytic work. Writing of the graphics she states:

Given the worldwide life threatening deterioration of the circumstances in which children are expected to live their lives, it could be argued that the greatest advancement human beings could make in the 21st century is to ensure the survival of their children. The construction of these graphics provides many opportunities to think about the dynamic complexity of the work that must be done to make the planet a child safe zone.

She has used the graphics to:

- Advocate that the support of children's emotional and physical well-being, and academic development should be a global priority;
- Argue that we have an ethical and moral responsibility to provide opportunities for every child to recover from trauma;
- Raise awareness of the ways policy decisions made locally, nationally and globally impact the health and well-being of children.

Early graphics (1973 -1993), which are not represented here focused on: (1) the social contexts in which literacy is central to children's problem solving; and (2) the complex ways in which literacy is used to enable and disable both children and people who have been marginalized in society.

The seven transdisciplinary graphics that followed (1993 – 2006) used literacy as an organizing principle. Each literacy graphic in this series undermines the assumptions that frame the thinking of political and corporate leaders and in many societies. Rather than Cartesian and linear the relationships in these literacy graphics are depicted as conditional and contingent.

The next two graphics focus on the social, political and economic discrimination in the education of children and the connection is made between the U.S. education system and the continuation of human activity, which is negatively impacting the atmospheric and terrestrial stability of the planet.

The four graphics that follow use mass trauma as an organizing principle and focus on the impact of armed conflict on children. The emphasis is on first and long term responses to violent human activity and highlights the role that teachers can have as first responders.

The final set of graphics (2006-2013) use human activity as an organizing principle and take into consideration the following interrelated phenomena:

Human Activity + Extreme Inequality + Climate Change + Ecological Collapse + Armed Conflict + Public Health Emergencies

Denny Taylor is convinced that these graphics provide both policy makers and the public with an opportunity to reimagine the supercomplexity of the interrelationships between atmospheric and ecosystem stressors caused by human activity.

Fifty years of insights from teaching and forty years of disciplined and systematic transdisciplinary research support her contention that power brokers have brought the planet and its children to breaking point. But she is still hopeful that mothers and fathers will take up the call to protect their children, and that life on the planet will be transformed – kinder, more compassionate, with room for all.

Literacy as an Organizing Principle.

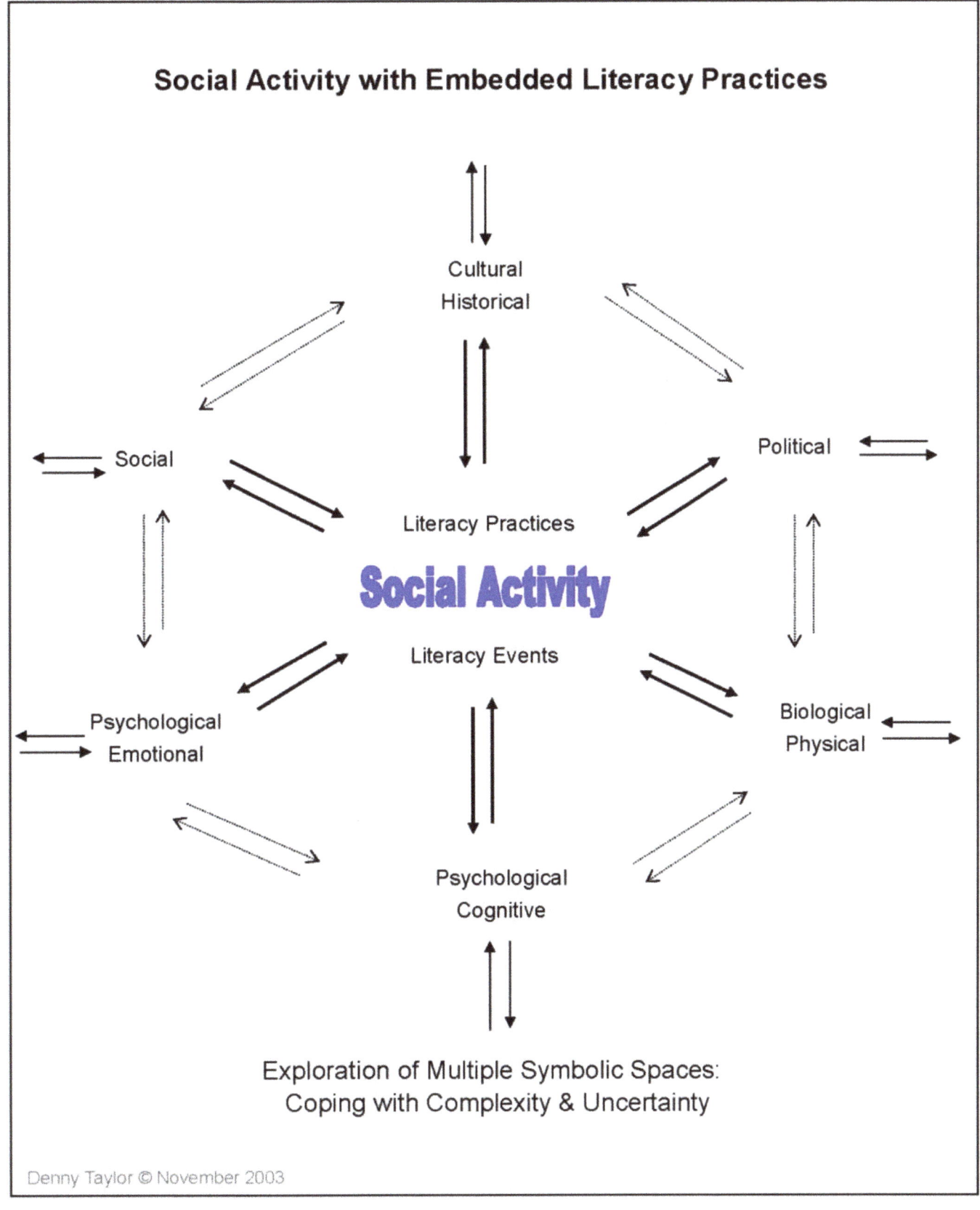

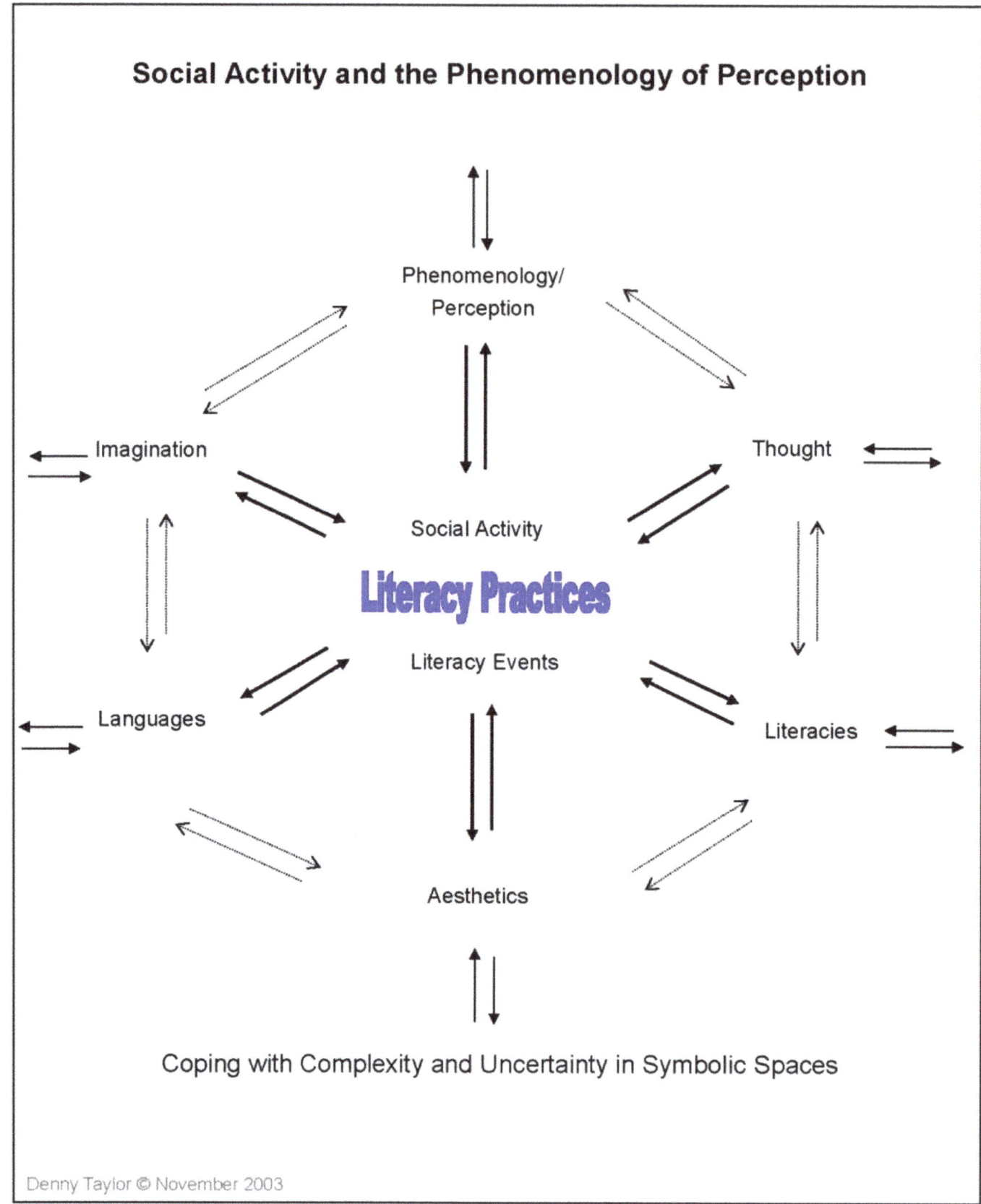

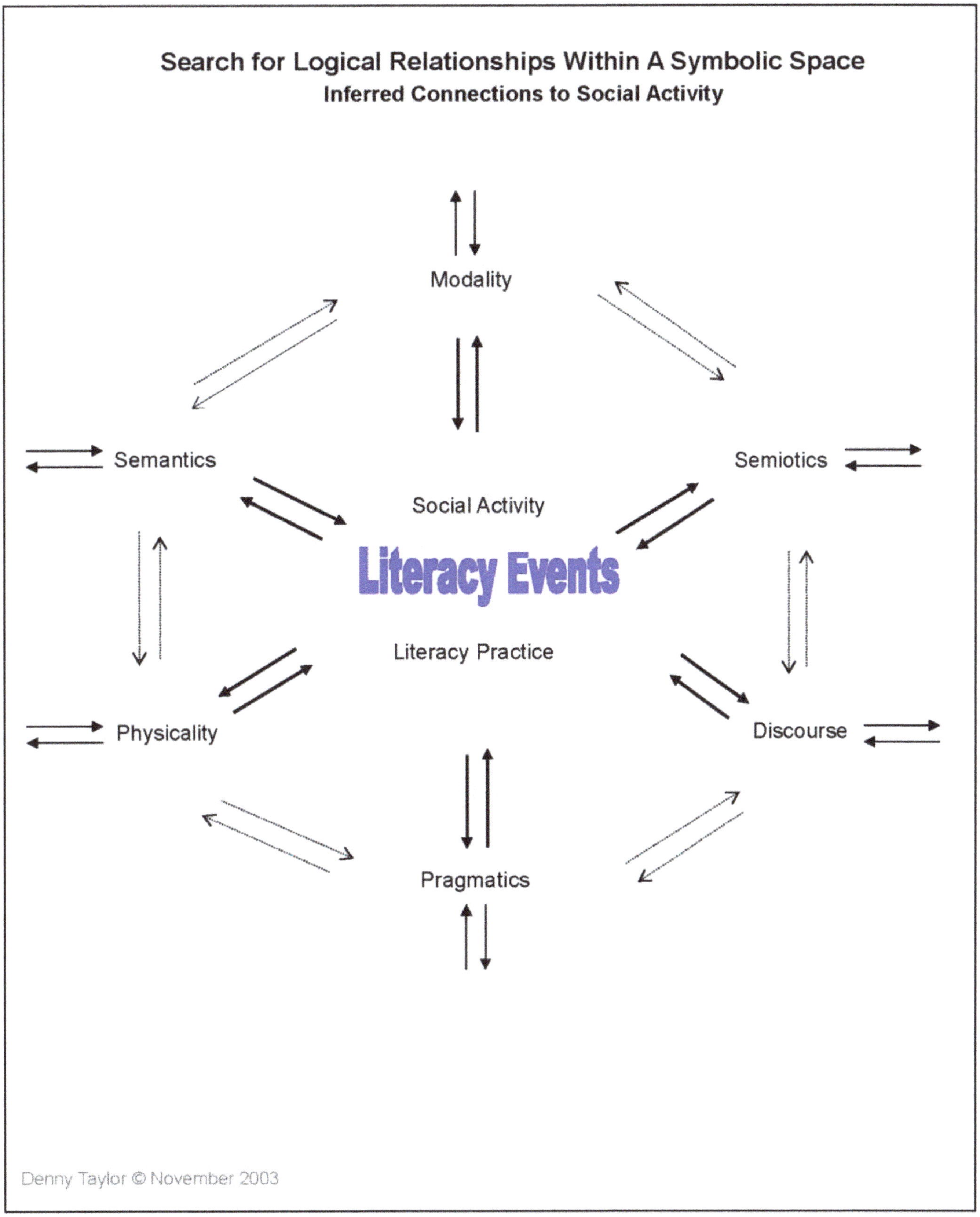

Search for Logical Relationships Within A Symbolic Space
Inferred Connections to Social Activity

Modality

Semantics

Semiotics

Social Activity

Literacy Events

Literacy Practice

Physicality

Discourse

Pragmatics

Denny Taylor © November 2003

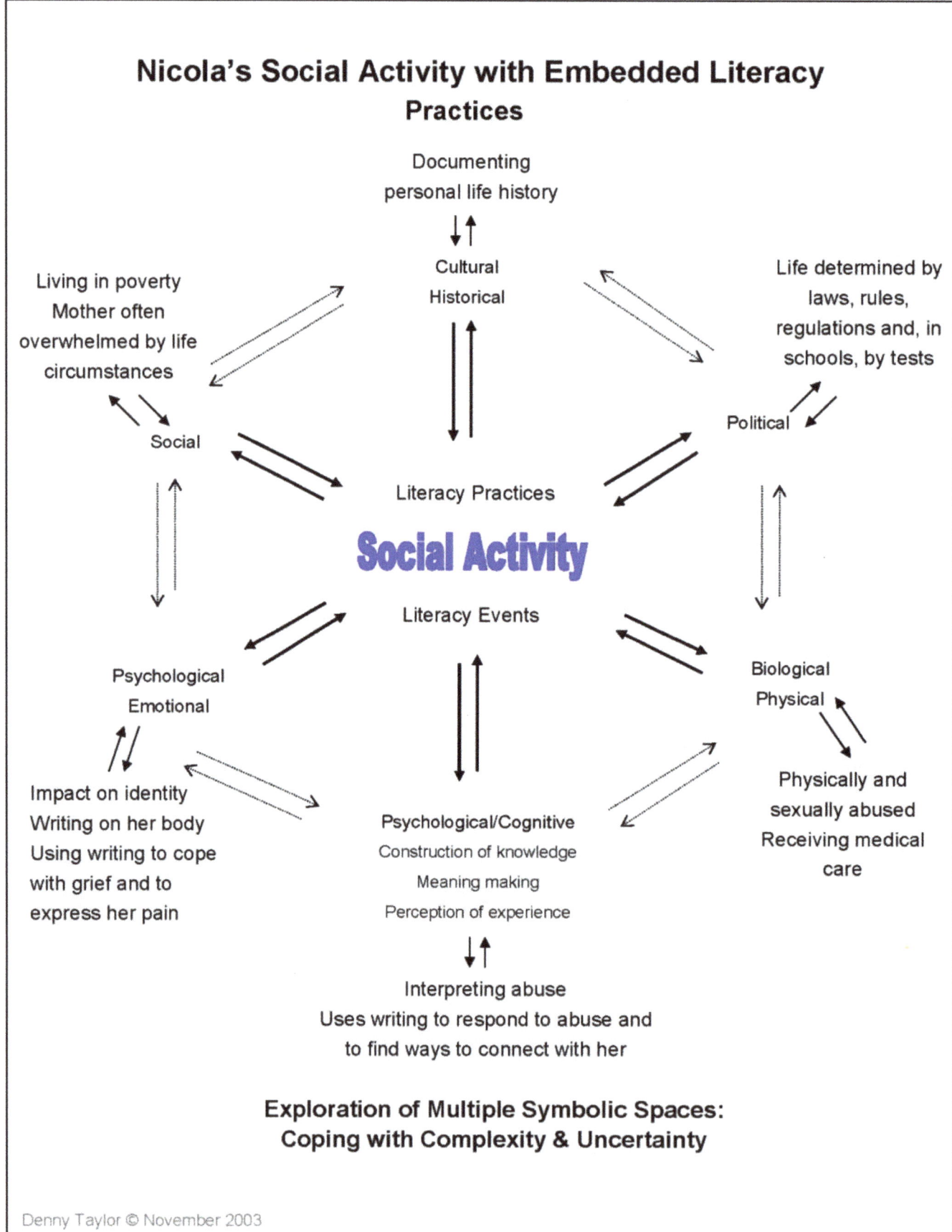

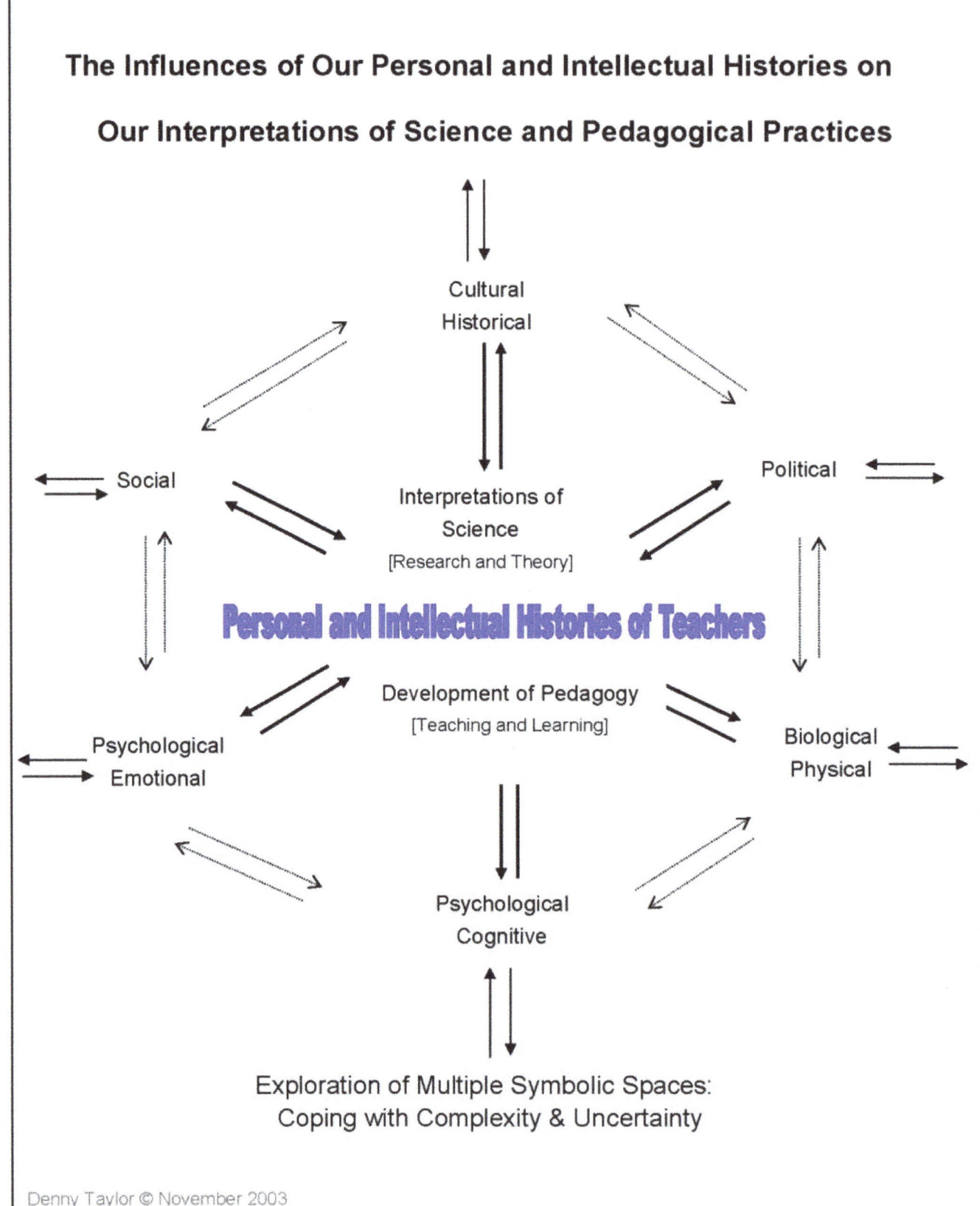

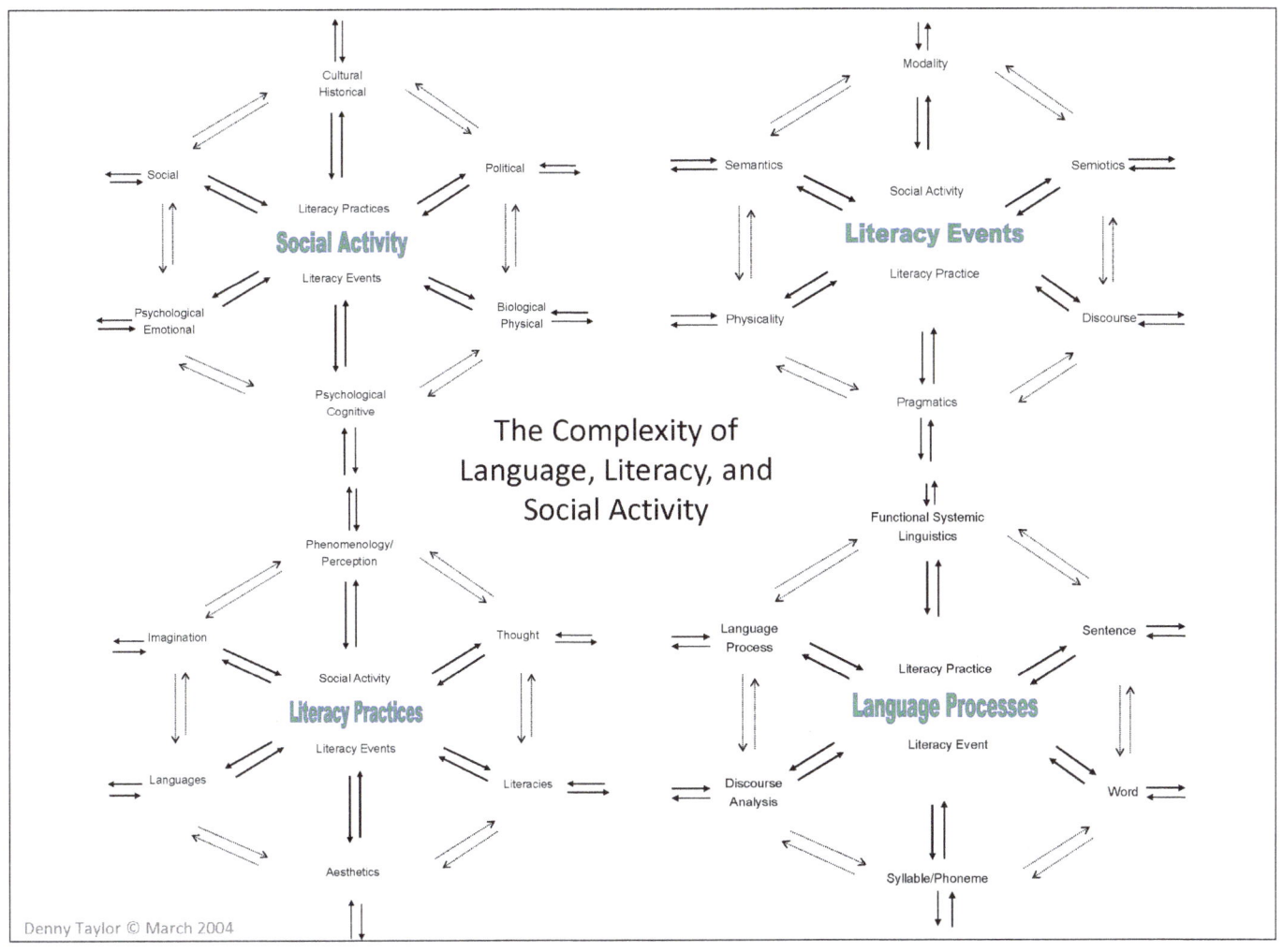

Social, Political, and Economic Discrimination in the Education of Children in the U.S.

Denny Taylor © October 2010

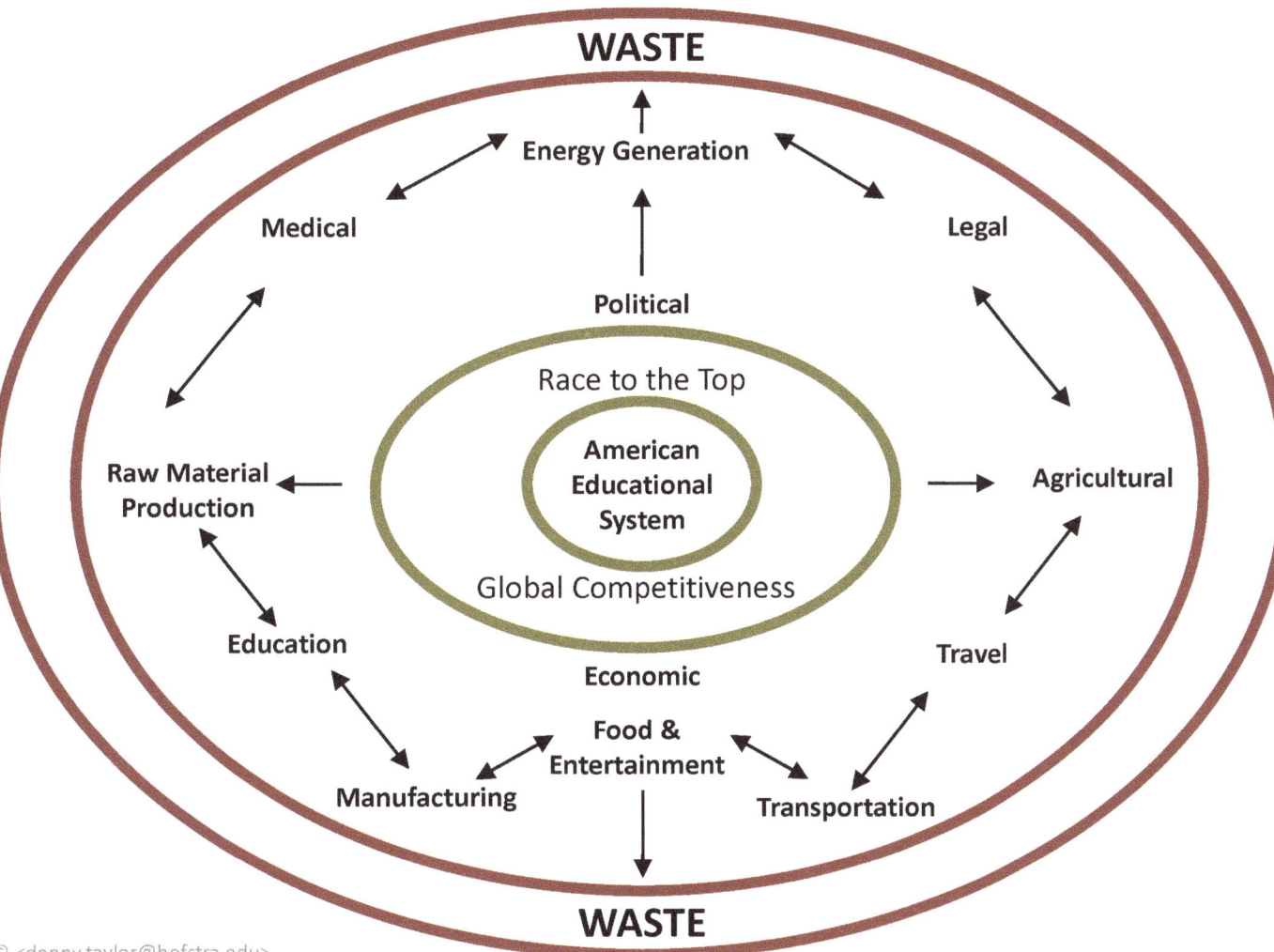

Trauma as an Organizing Principle Teachers as First Responders Supporting Children in Regions of Armed Conflict and Catastrophic Events.

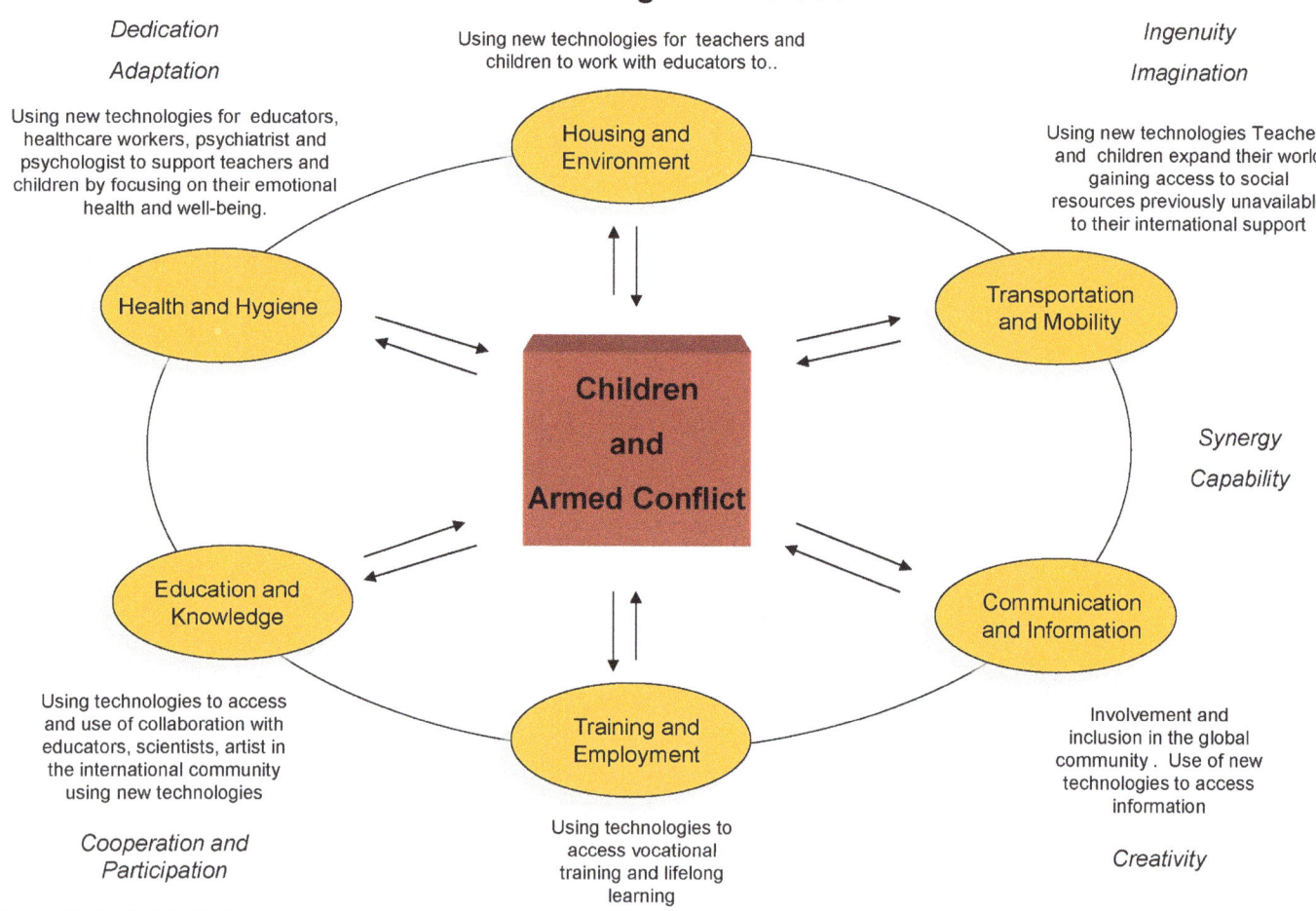

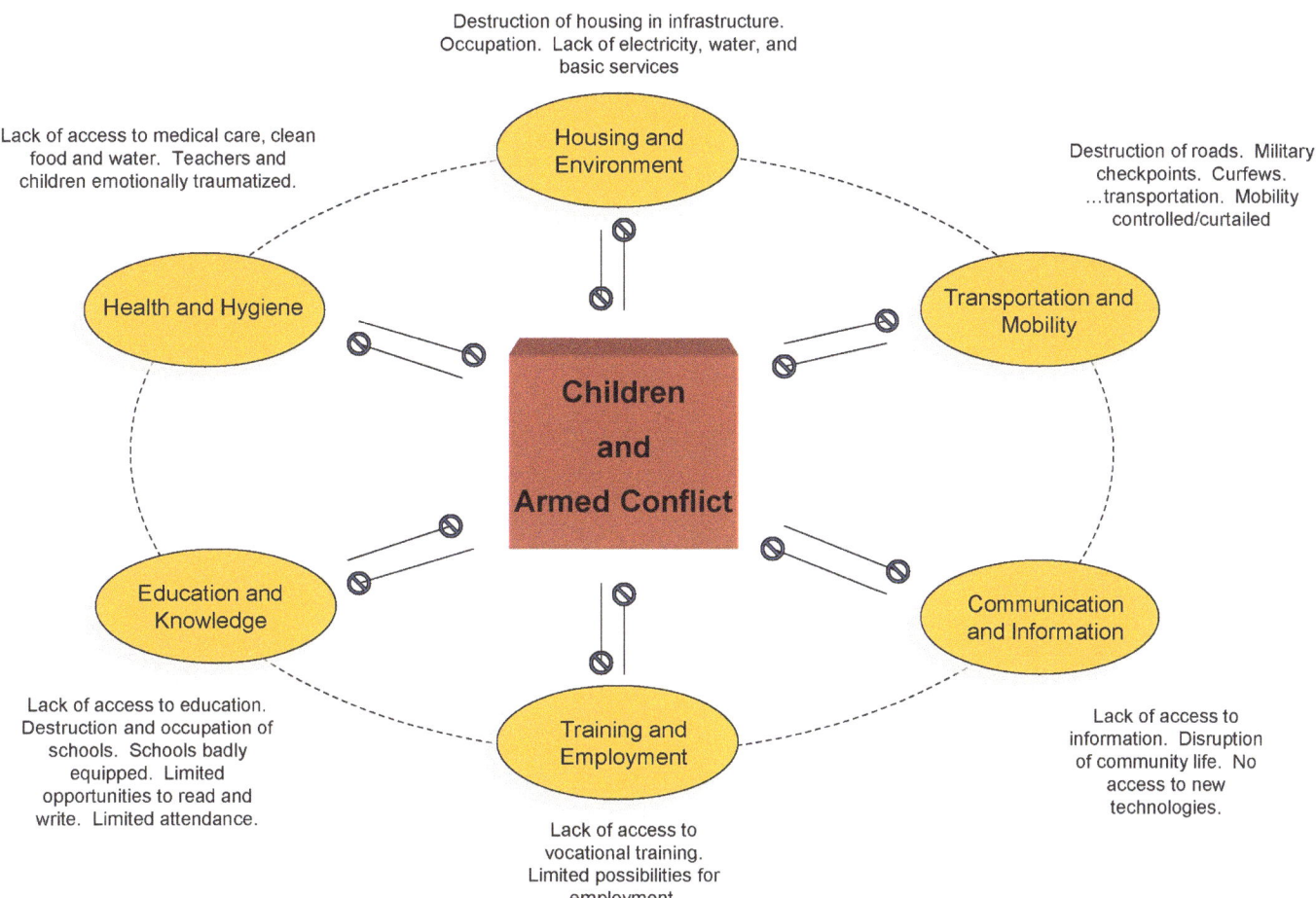

Teachers Helping Teachers: Overcoming Social Exclusion Using Scientific and Technological Innovation

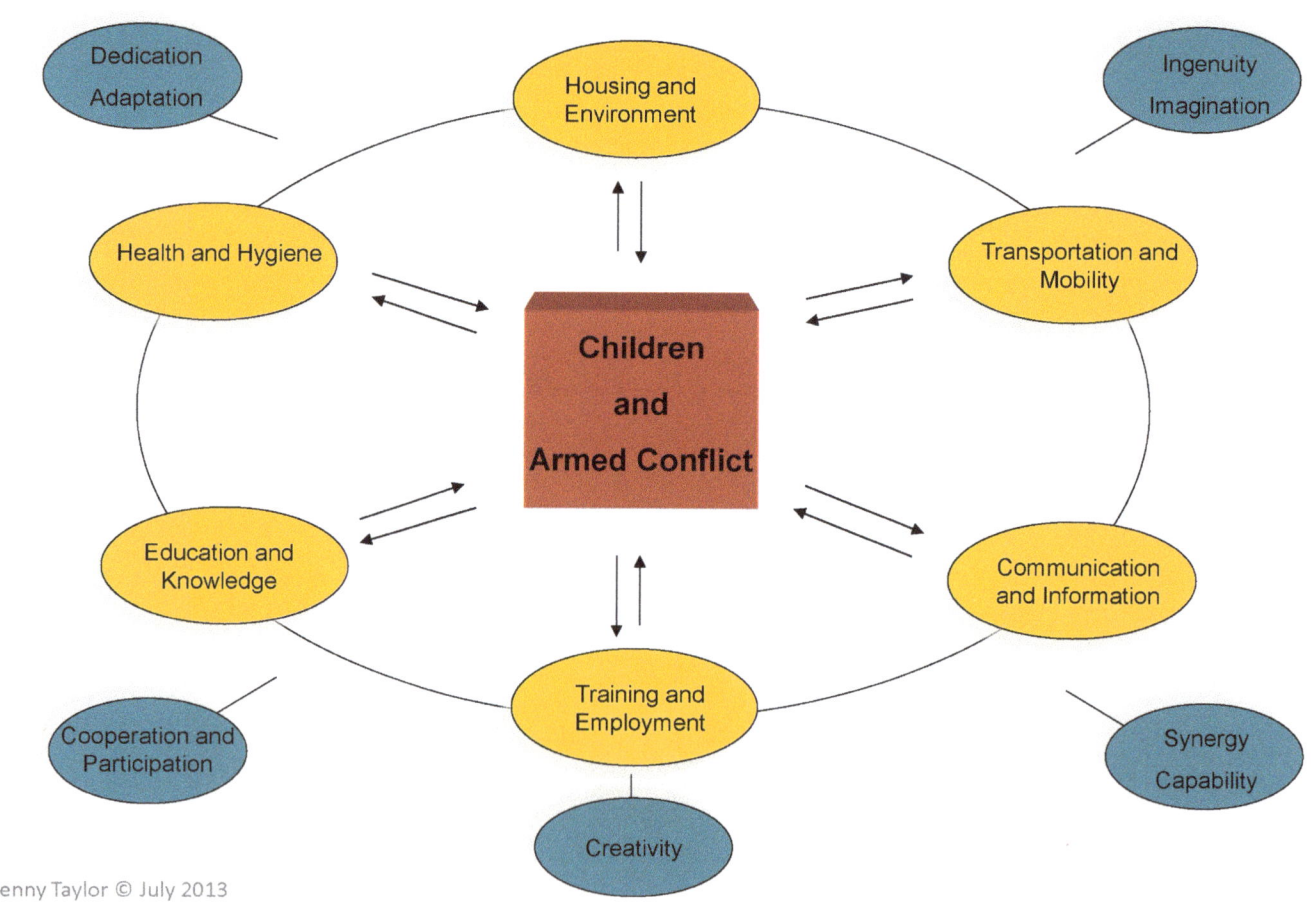

The research increasingly focuses on children and catastrophic events.

Inevitably this work has resulted in the consideration of climate change and the study of Earth system science.

The Impact of Human Activity on the Planet as an Organizing Principle.

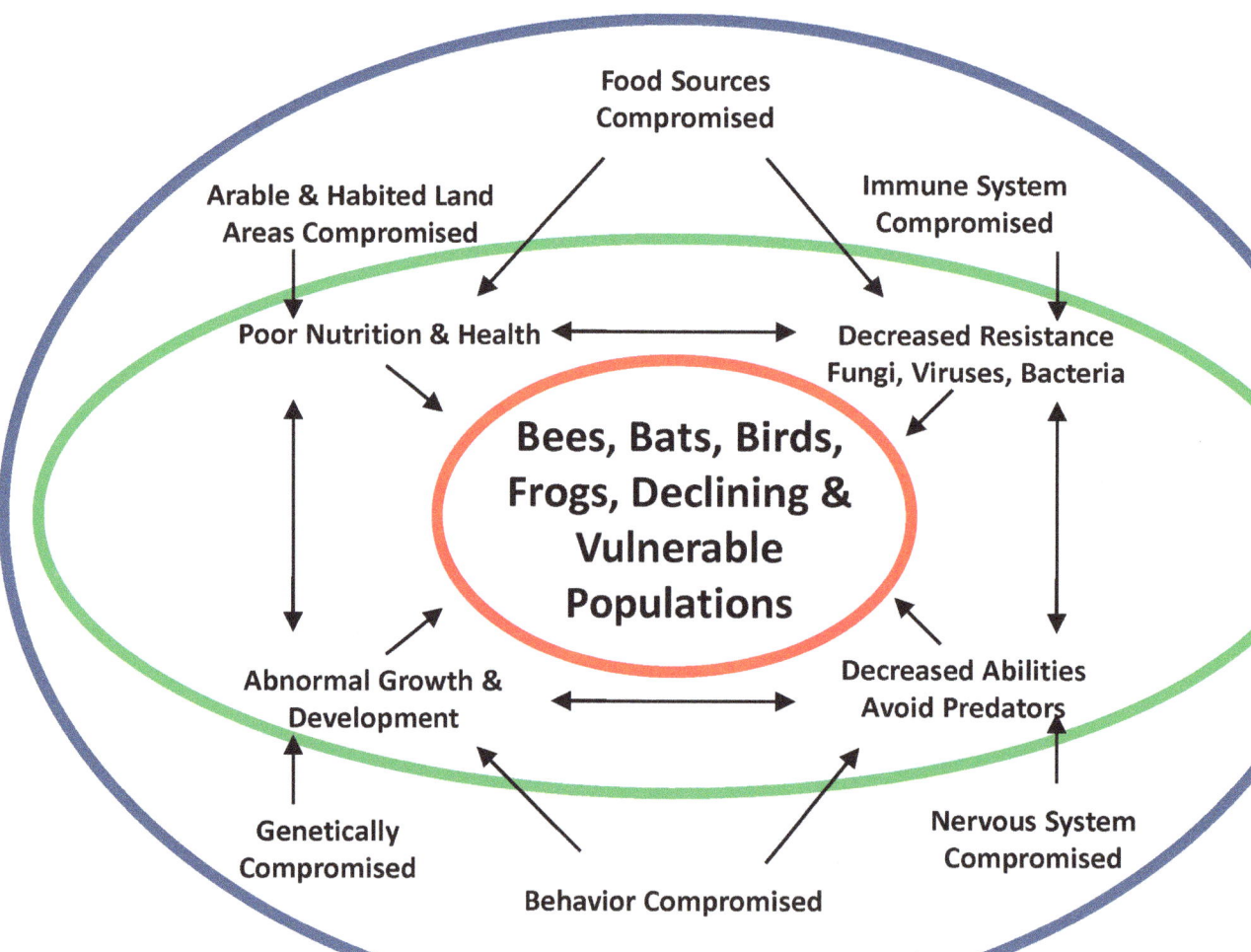

Denny Taylor © October 2010

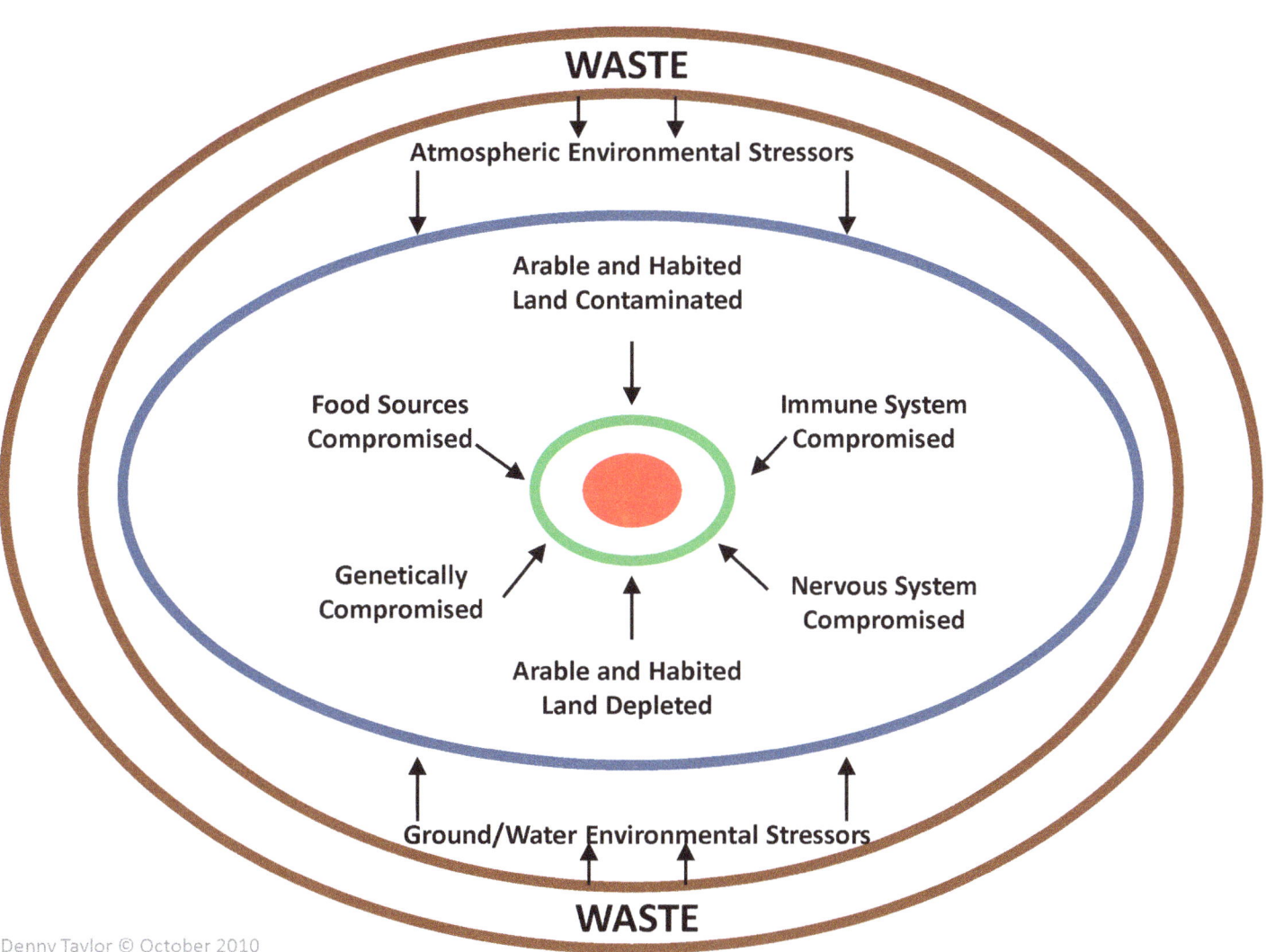

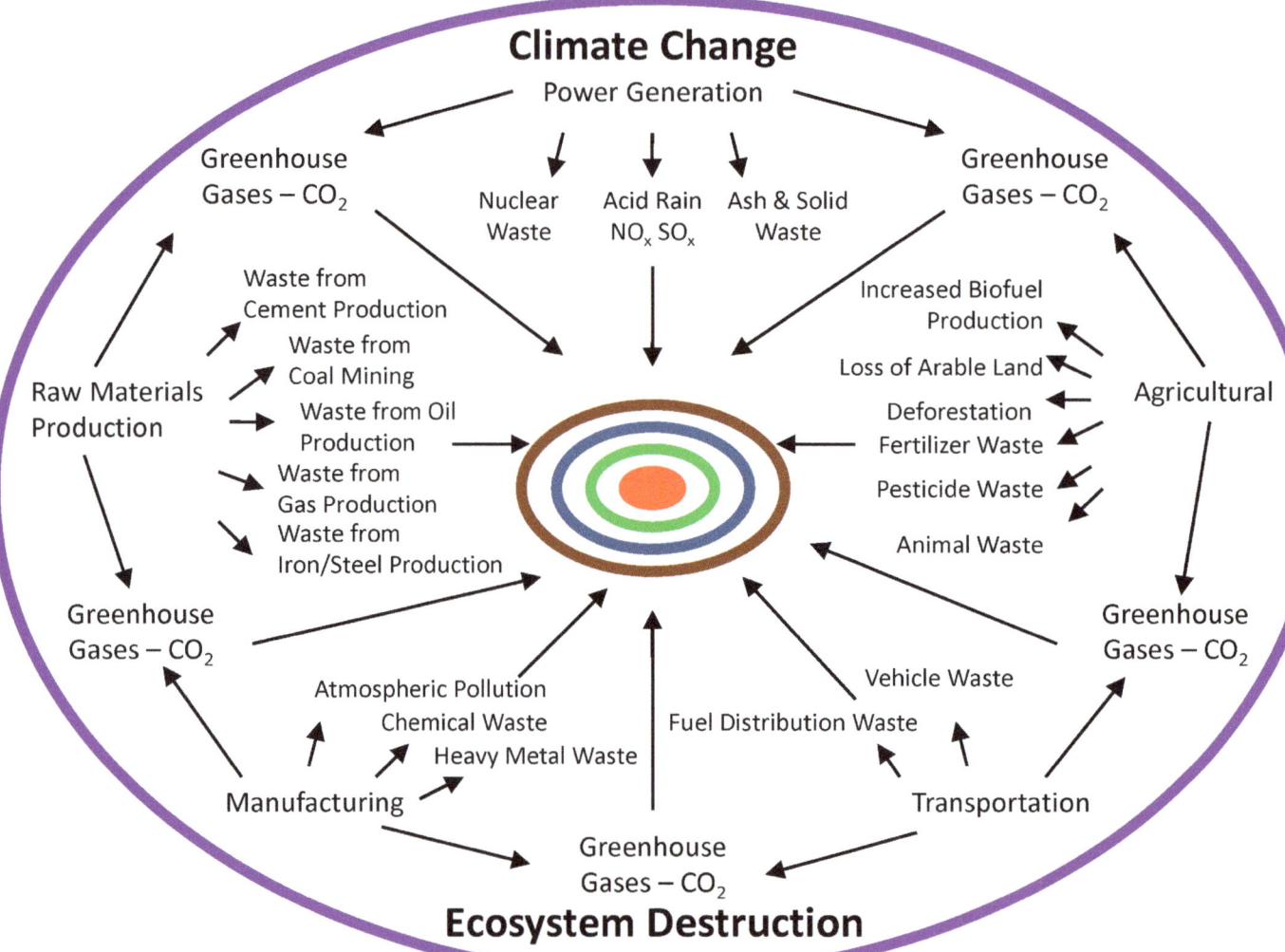

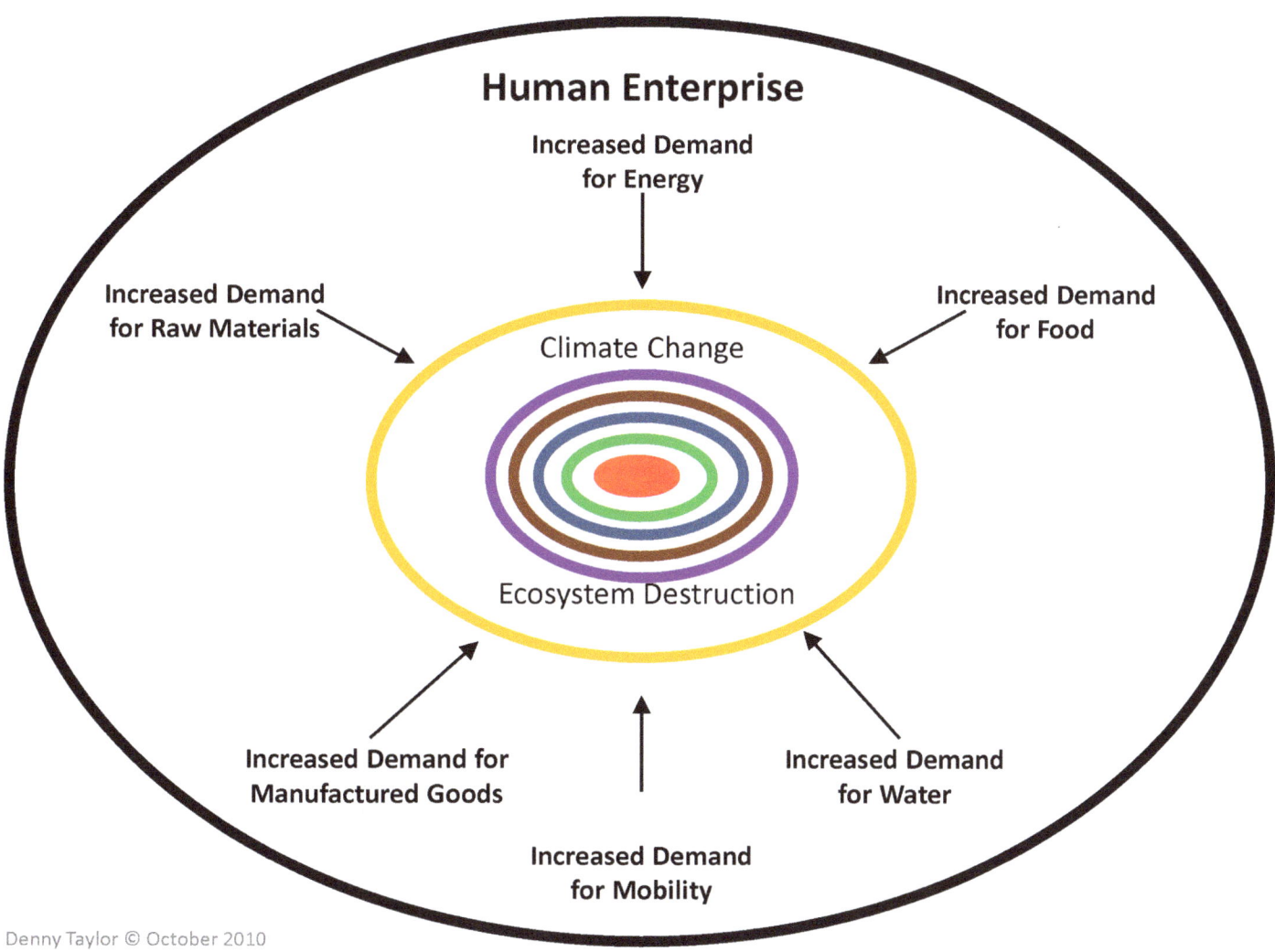

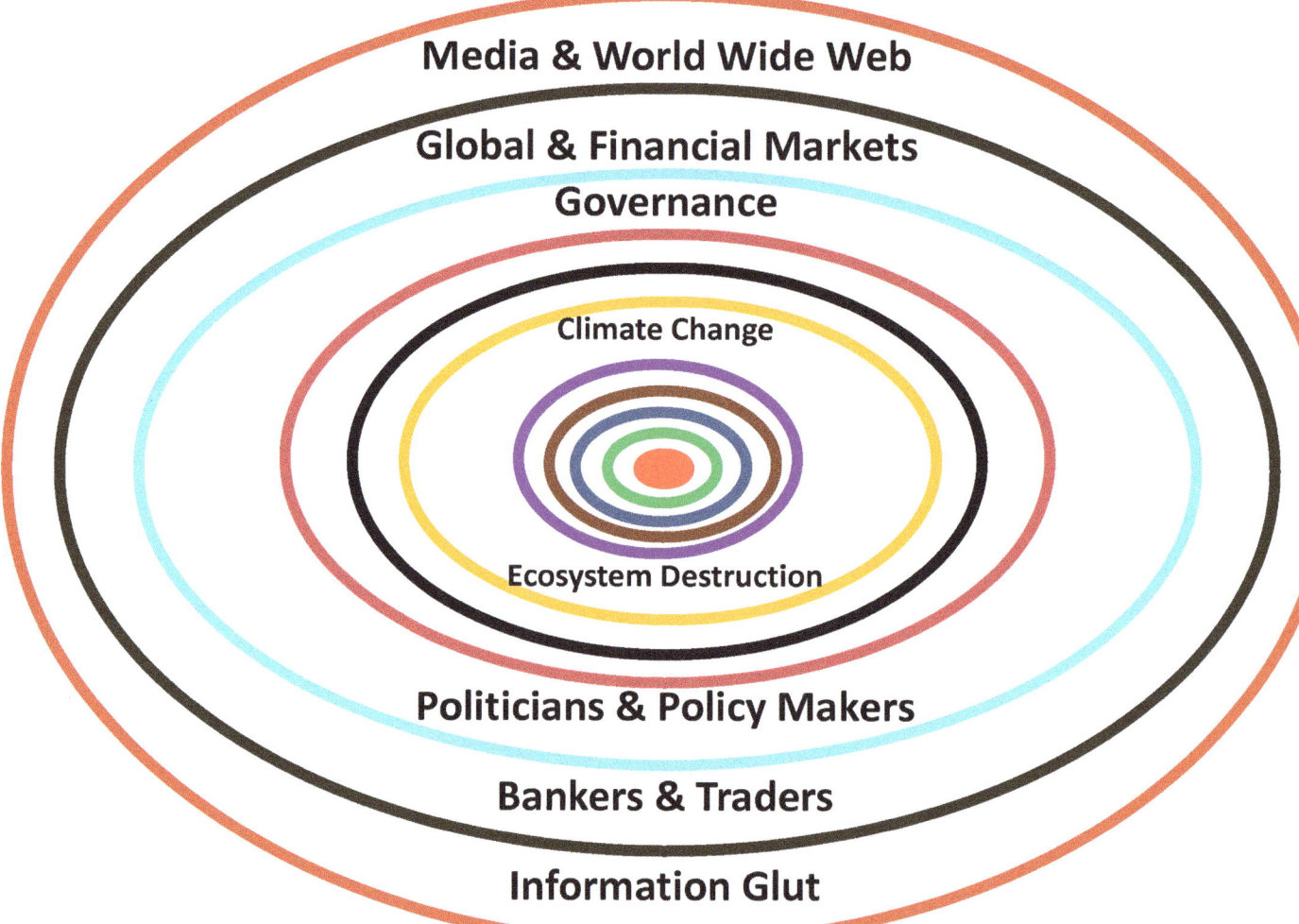

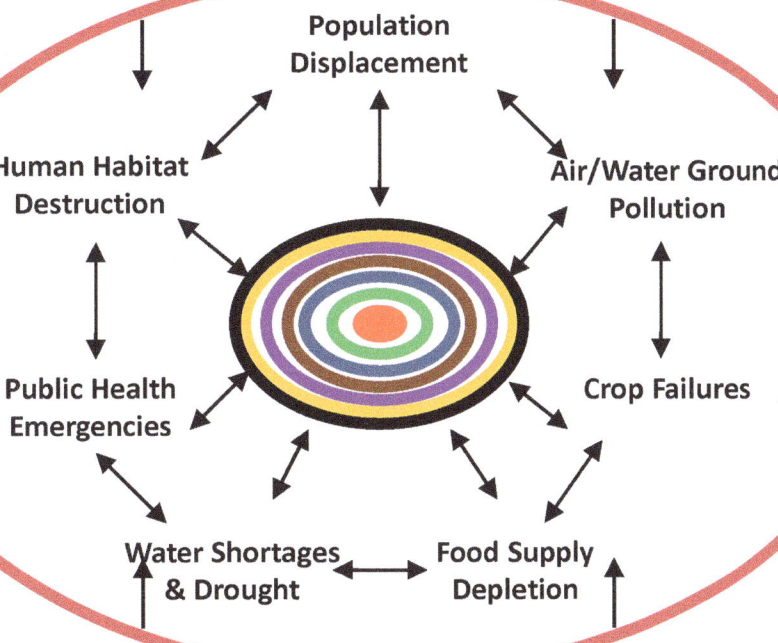

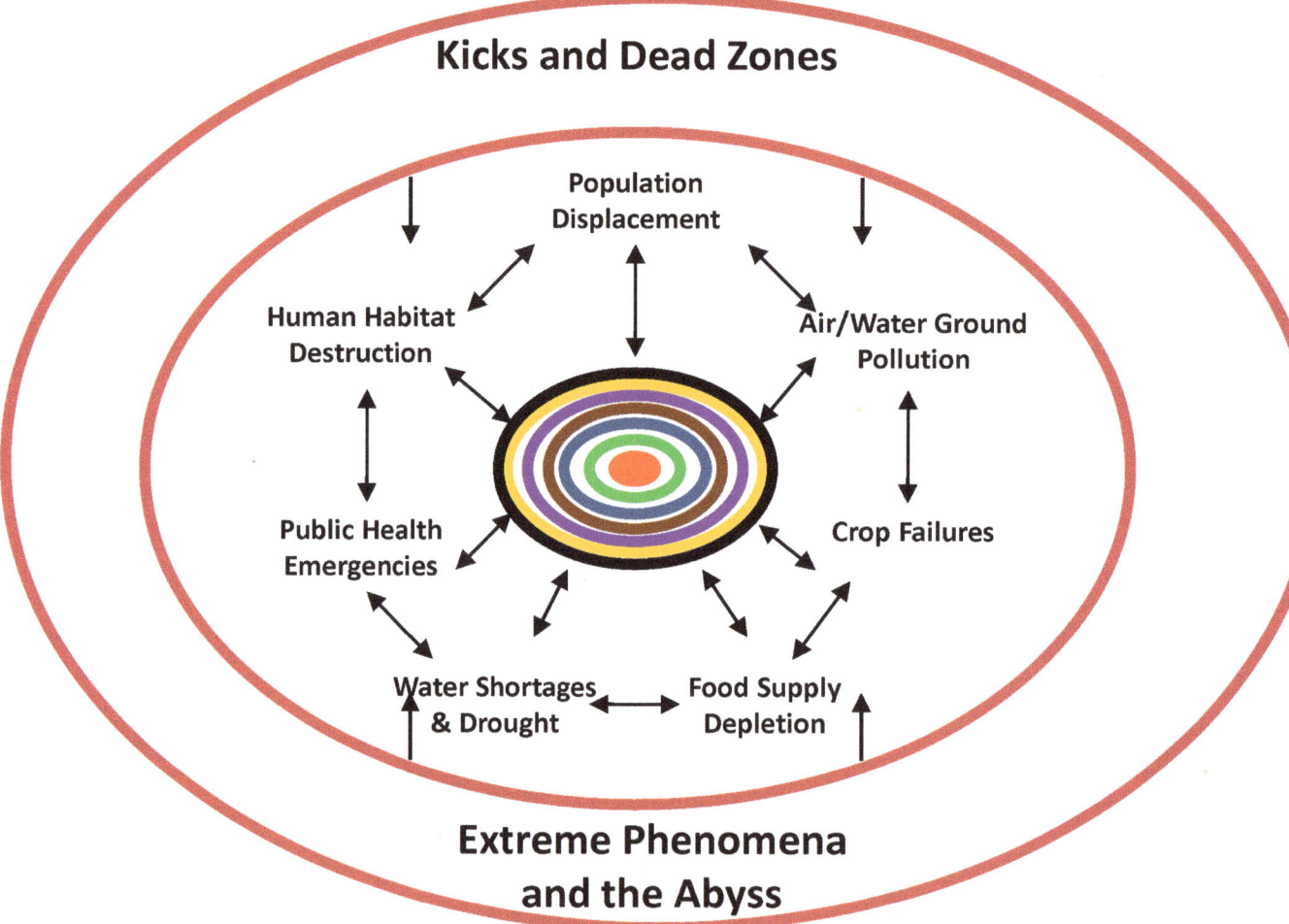

Extreme Weather Events

- Population Displacement
- Air/Water Ground Pollution
- Crop Failures
- Food Supply Depletion
- Water Shortages & Drought
- Public Health Emergencies
- Human Habitat Destruction

Social Unrest and Armed Conflict

Denny Taylor © October 2010

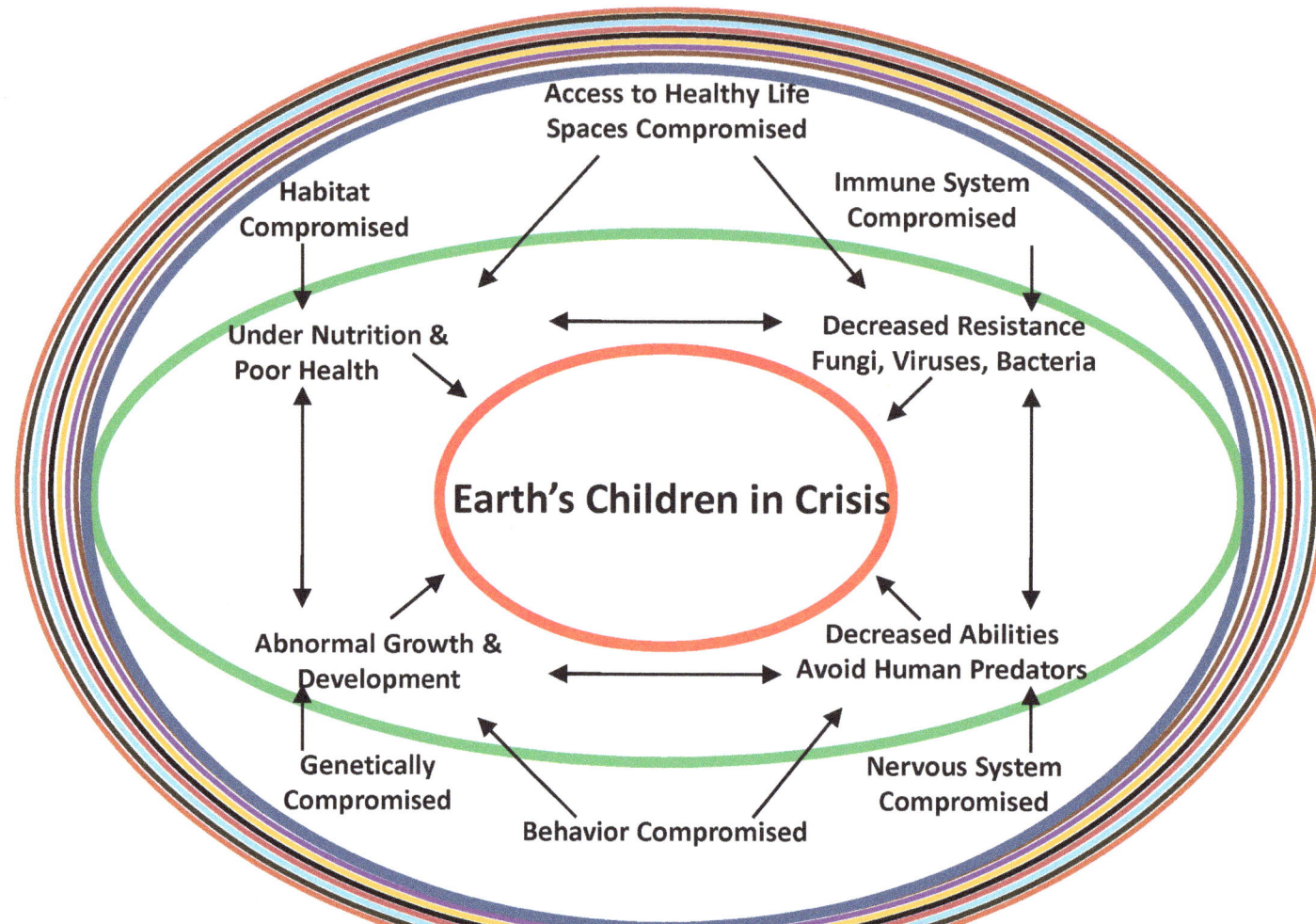

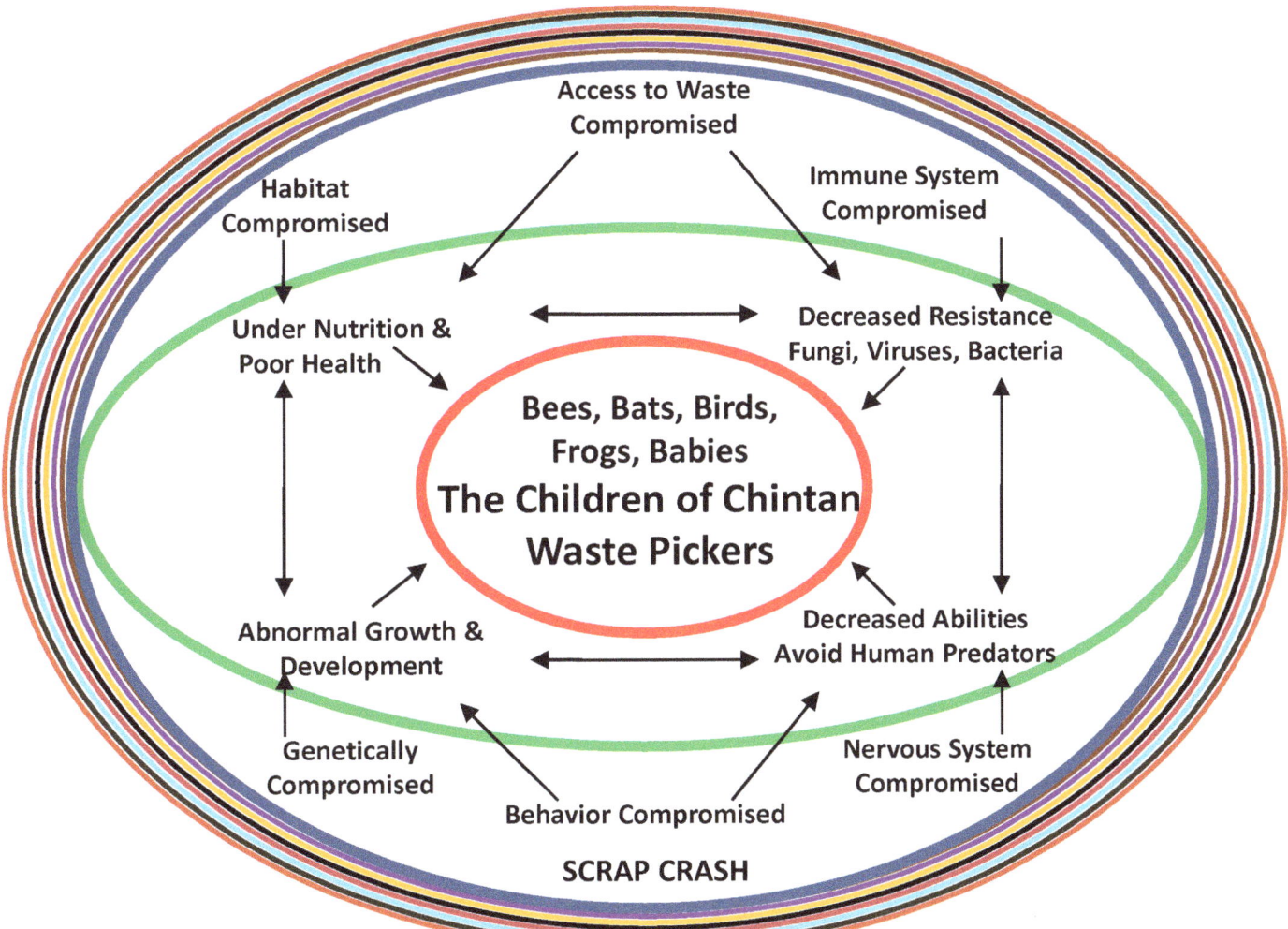

Bhopal: The Social, Economic, and Ecological Cost of Industrial Disasters.

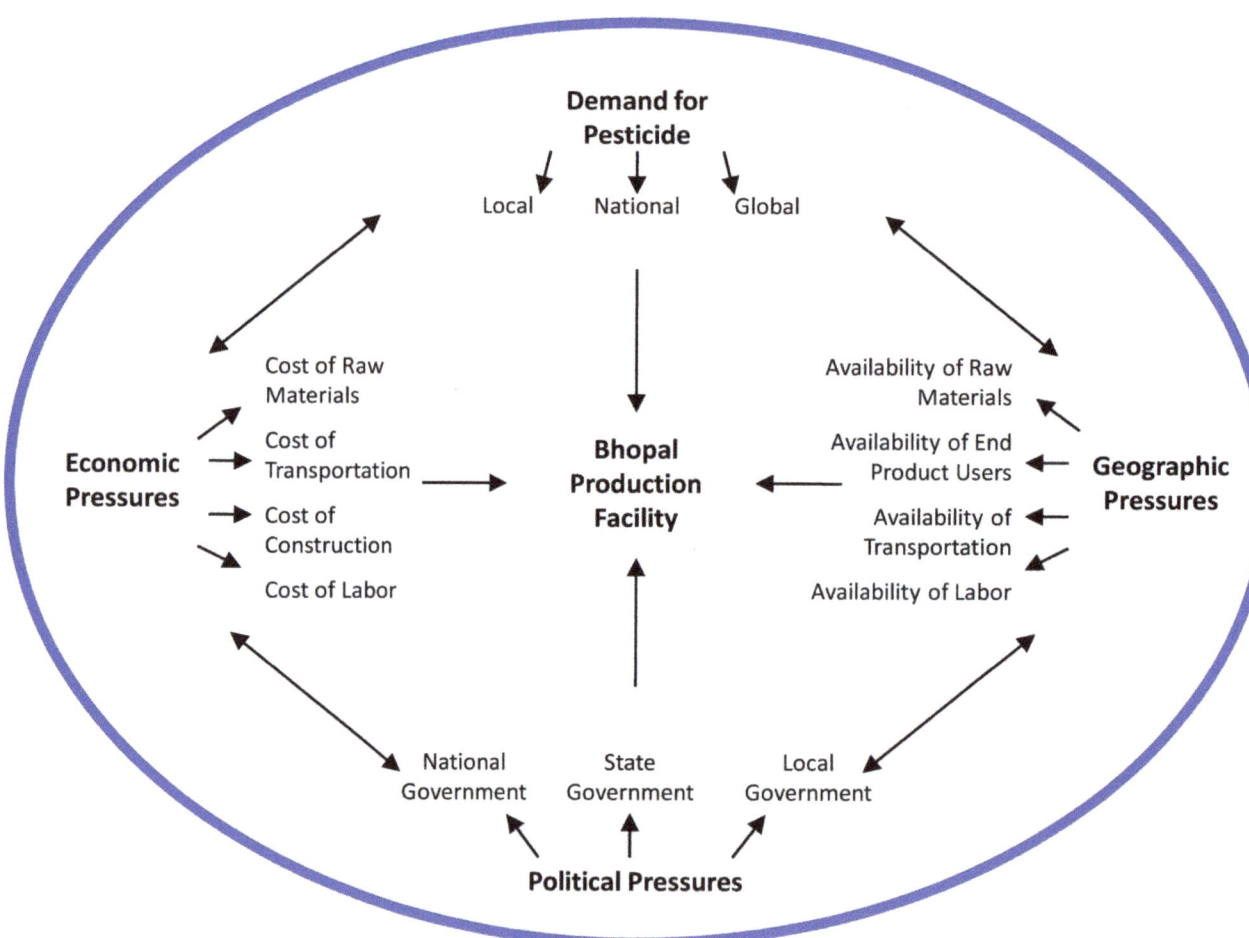

Denny Taylor © October 2010

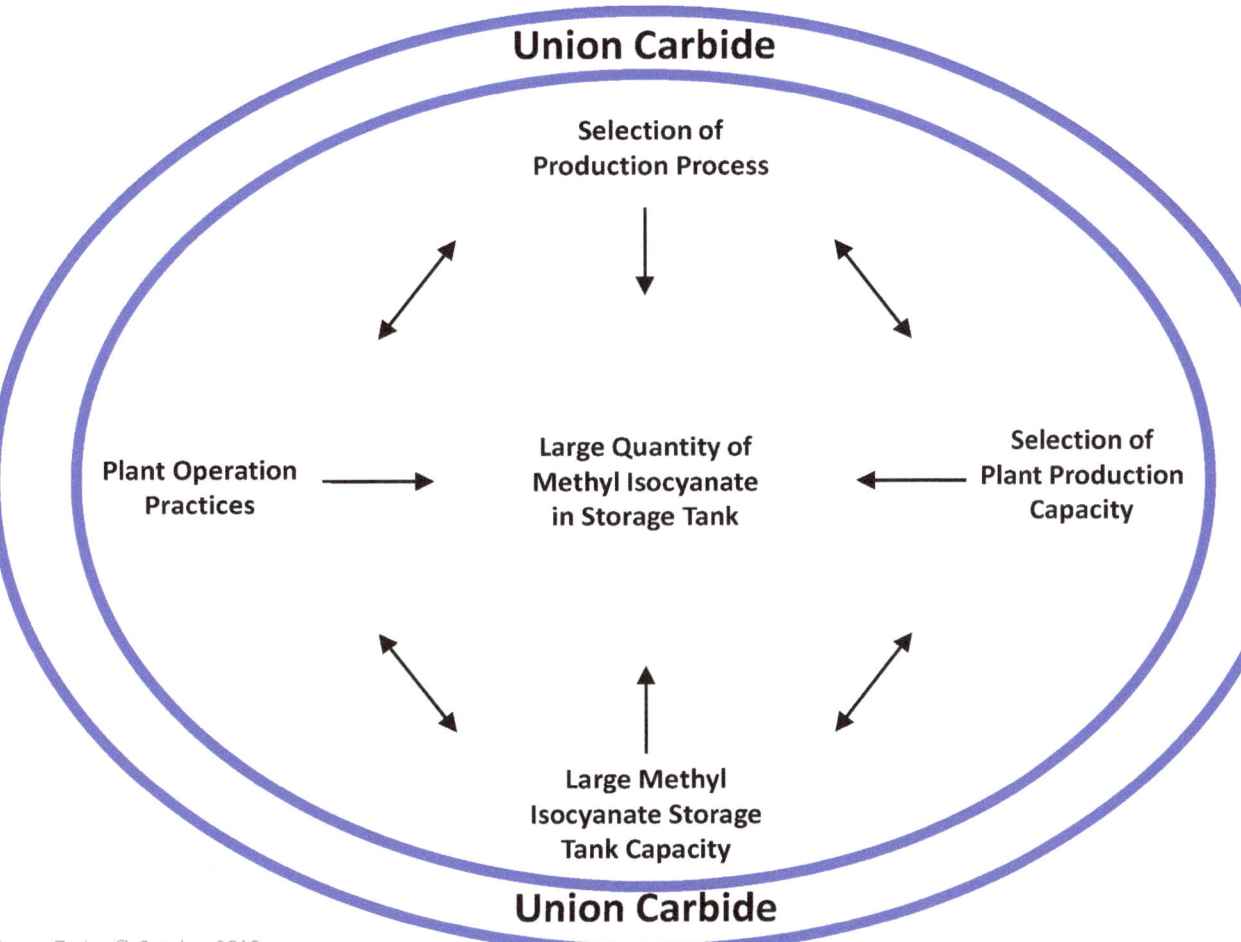

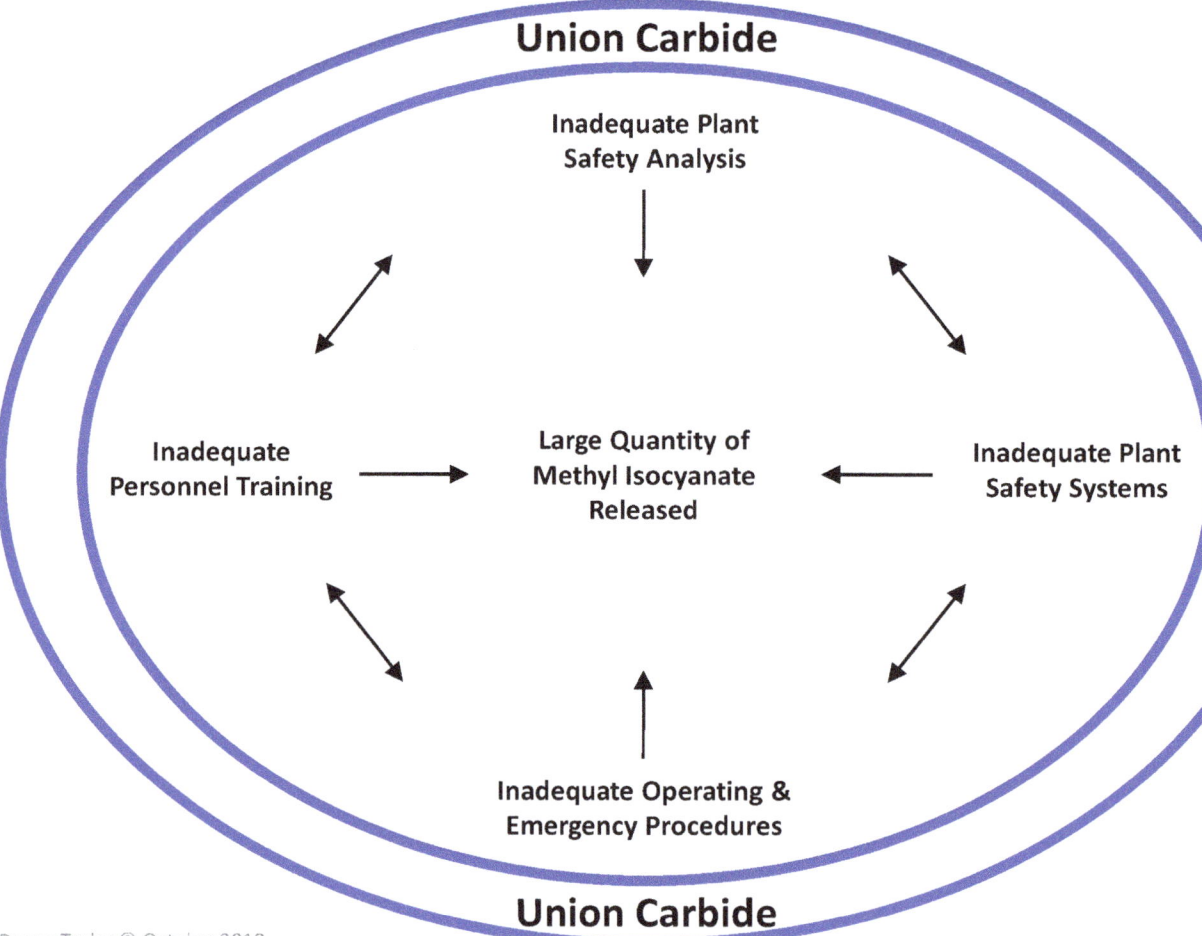

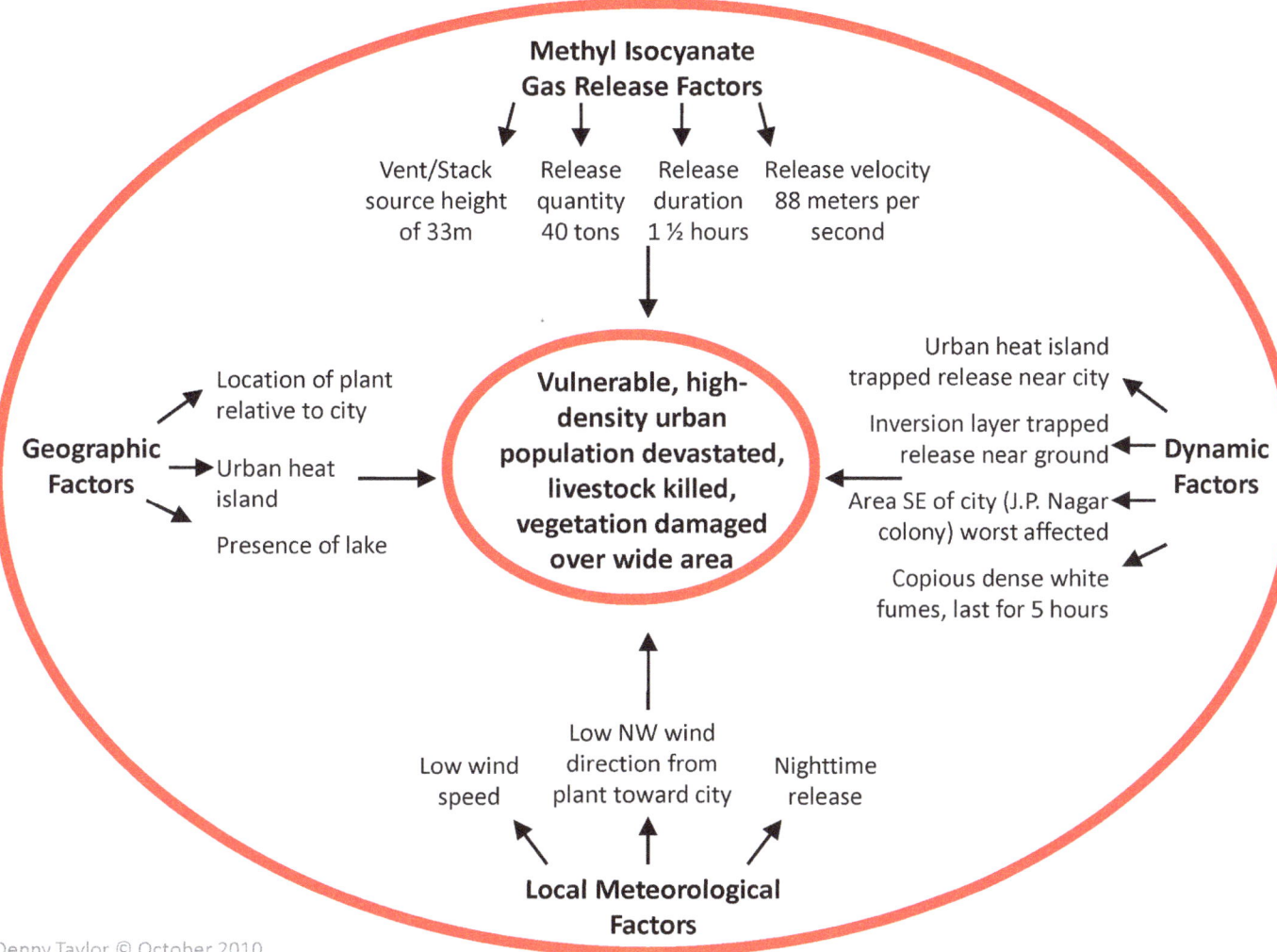

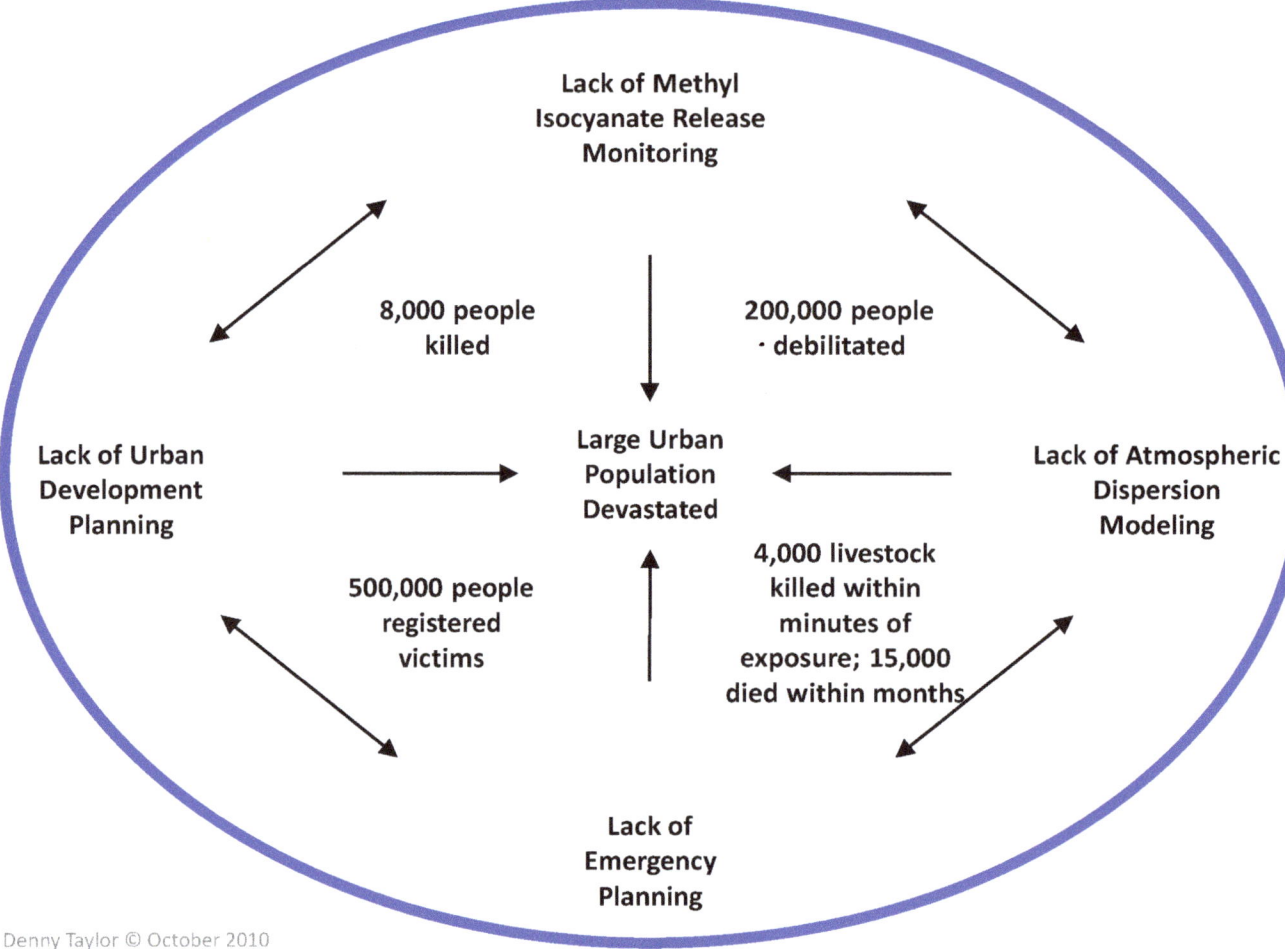

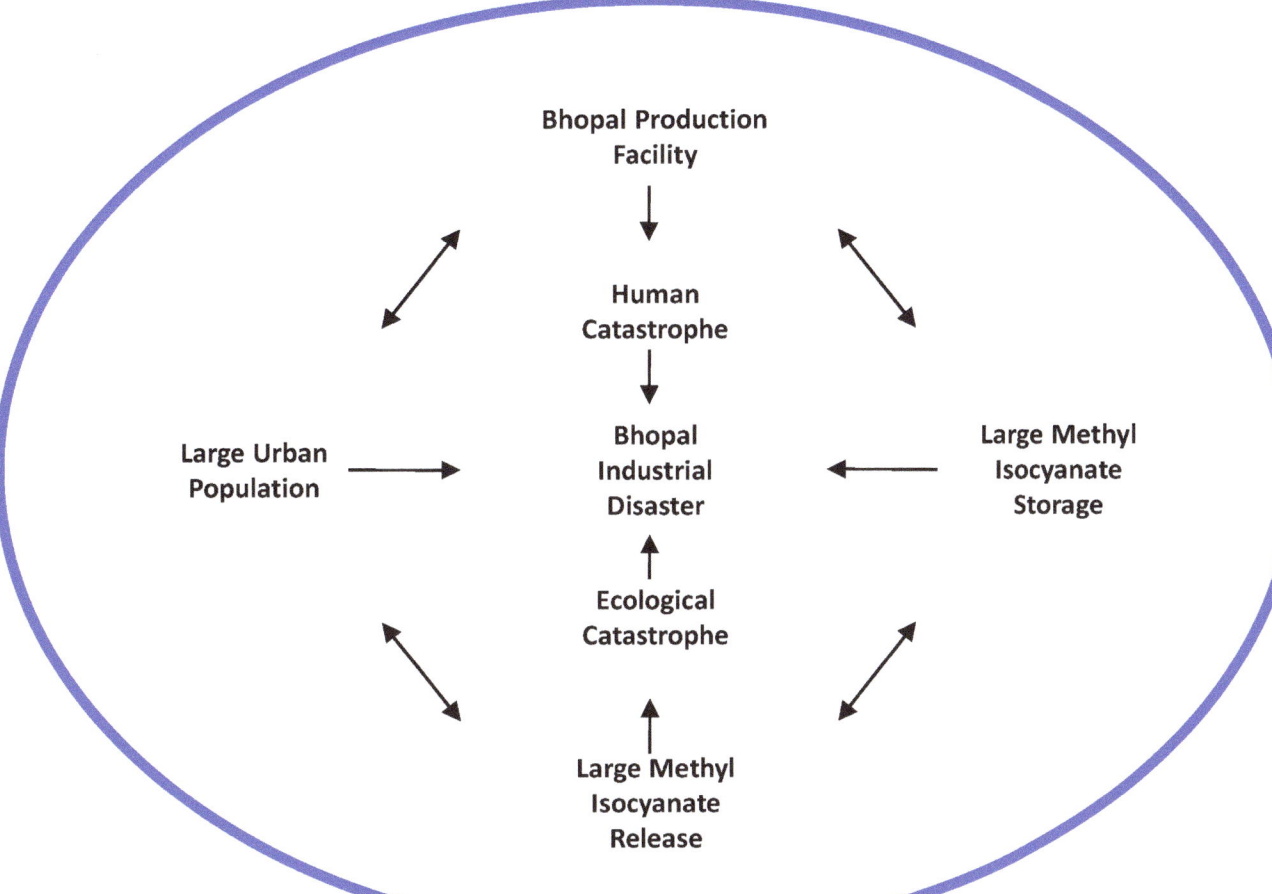

BP Gulf Ecosystem Destruction Terrestrial and Marine Ecosystems Lost or Compromised.

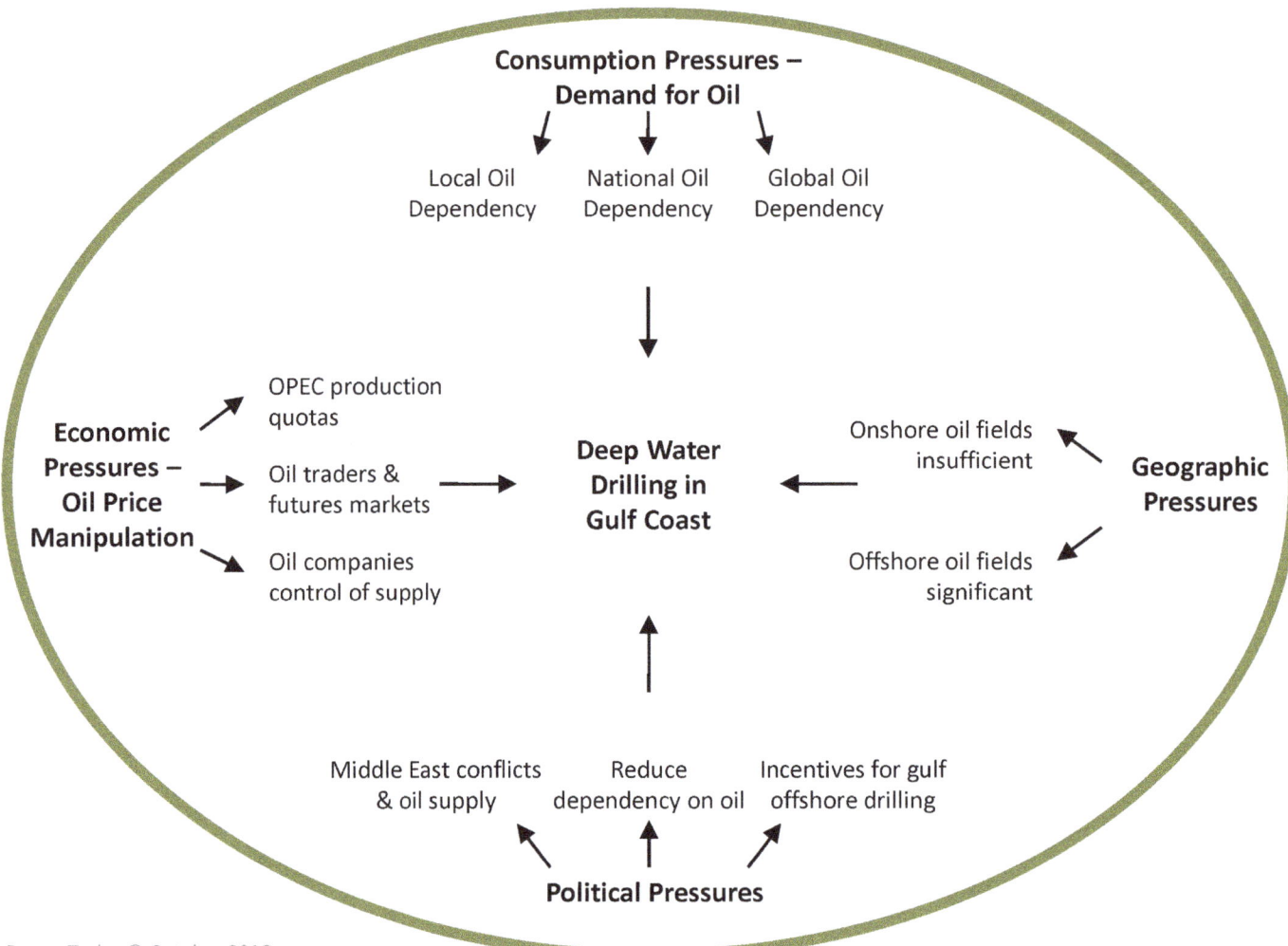

Denny Taylor © October 2010

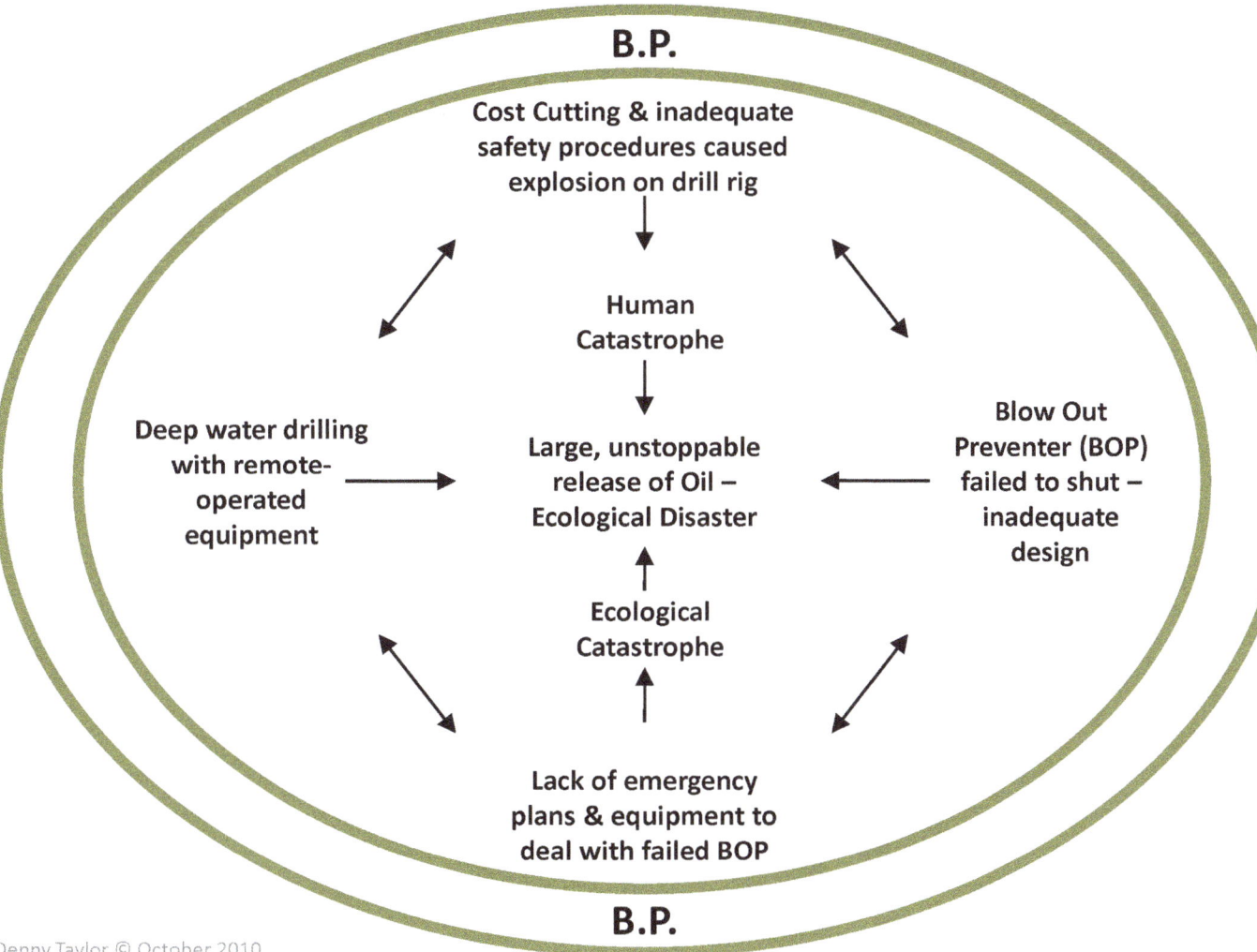

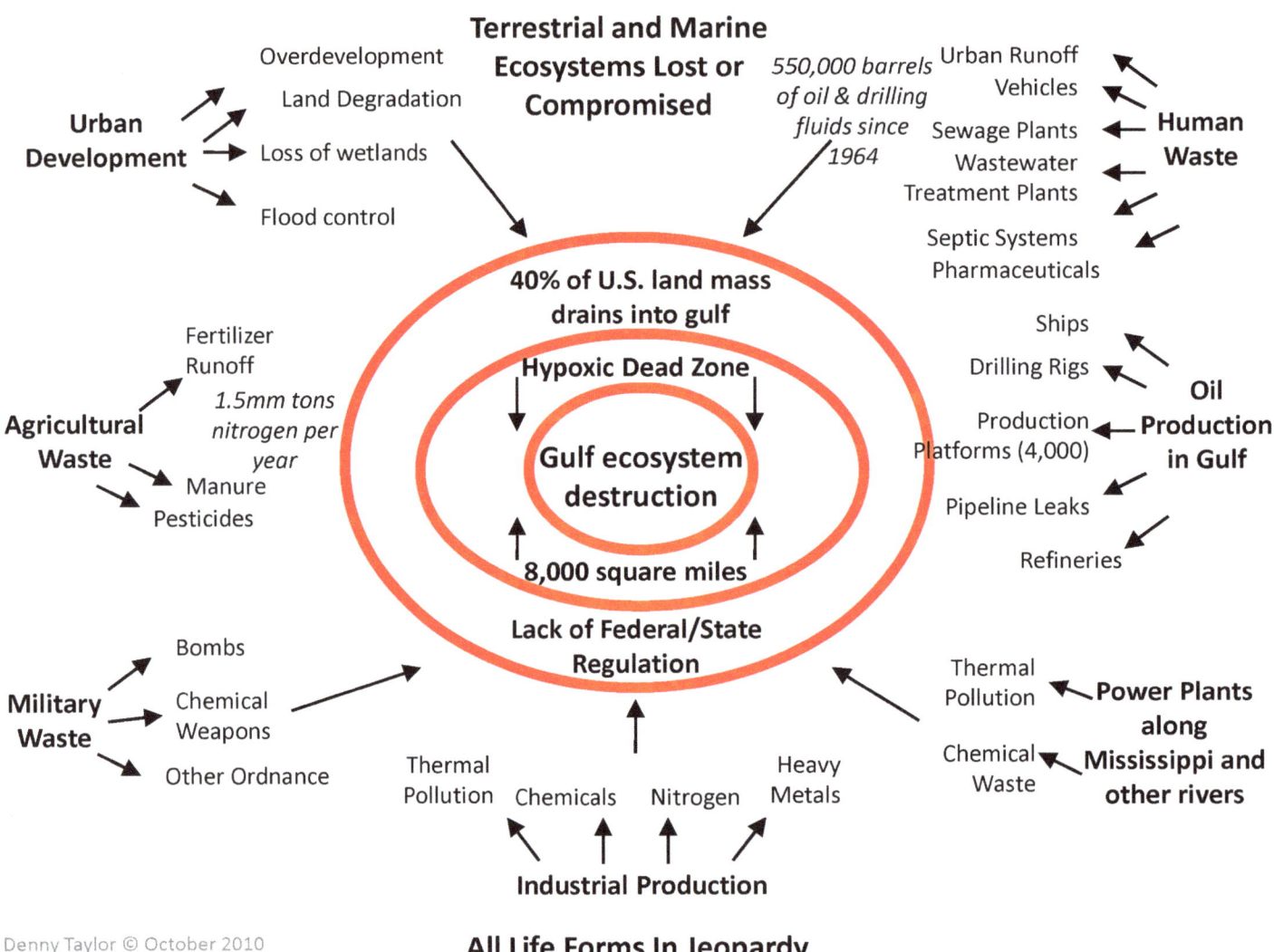

Rapid Increase in Existential Risks Future Generations in Jeopardy.

Denny (Denalene) Taylor: Curriculum Vitae Summary.

Education

Doctoral Degree: Columbia University: January, 1981 (Transdisciplinary Research Combining Anthropology, Sociology, Psychology and Education)

Master of Arts: Columbia University: June 1980

Master of Education in the Psychology of Reading: Rutgers University, June 1977

Teachers Certificate: Fine Art and Early Childhood Education: Roehampton University (formerly Whitelands College), London, August 1968

Enduring Transdisciplinary Research Question

If we include consideration for the health and well-being of everybody's child in our response to the global crises that are taking place, how would that affect our present and future actions?

In response to this question all research endeavors across disciplines, paradigms and fields, focus on the complex interrelationships between: Children and their Families + Climate Change + the Ecological Crisis + the Global Economic Crisis + Armed Conflict + Public Health Emergencies + Extreme Poverty.

Books (+100,000 sold)

Toodle-oo Ruby Blue! (2107); *Split Second Solution* (2016); *Rat-a-tat-tat! I've Lost My Cat!* (2015); *Rosie's Umbrella* (2015; Second Edition, 2017); *Nineteen Clues: Great Transformations Can Be Achieved Through Collective Action* (2014); *Save Our Children, Save Our School, Pearson Broke the Golden Rule*, (2014); *Beginning to Read and the Spin Doctors of Science*, (1998); *Many Families, Many Literacies: An International Declaration of Principles*, editor, (1997); *Teaching and Advocacy*, co-editor, (1997); *Toxic Literacies: Exposing the Injustice of Bureaucratic Texts*, (1996); *From The Child's Point Of View*, (1993); *Learning Denied: Inappropriate Educational Decision Making*, (1990); *Growing Up Literate, Learning From Inner City Families*, co-authored (1988); *Family Storybook Reading*, co-authored, (1986); *Family Literacy: Young Children Learning to Read and Write*, (1983); Second Edition, September (1998)

Scholarly Writing

19 peer-reviewed articles; 18 chapters; 8 reviews and forewords; 3 requested guest editorials: 10 transdisciplinary theoretical models (combining research in the social and physical sciences, and the humanities).

International and National Conference Presentations (Organizer; Invited Presenter)

46 keynotes; +100 International and national presentations

Transdisciplinary Presentations in the Social & Physical Sciences, & Humanities

Participant in the 2009 ICSU/ISSC On-Line Global Visioning Consultation; Participant in the 2010 ICSU/ISSC Open Visioning Consultation Forum, UNESCO, Paris, resulting in the publication of the *Grand Challenges Report*, which is a consensus list of the highest priorities for Earth system science that would remove critical barriers impeding progress toward sustainable development. (More than 1000 individuals from 85 countries contributed in the initial online consultation, and more than 200 individuals and 46 institutions reviewed the draft of the *Grand Challenges*.) *Planet Under Pressure Global Conference on Earth System Science*, London, 2012: 4 peer reviewed presentations accepted focusing on: (1) The State of the Planet; (2) Meeting Global Needs;(3) Transforming our way of living; & (4) Governing Across Scales.

Academic Positions, Research, & Teaching

Professor Emeritus of Literacy Studies, Hofstra University, 2013 -

Professor of Literacy Studies: Hofstra University, 1998-2013

Professor Plus: 2004; Second Tier 2010

Founder & Chair of the Literacy Studies Department: 1998-2004 (Re-conceptualized 11 masters degree programs and 3 doctoral degree programs)

Founder & Doctoral Director of Literacy Studies: 1998-2010 (Dissertation Chair +25 students)

Founder & Director of the International Center for Everybody's Child at Hofstra University: 2005. Formally approved by the President of Hofstra, 2008.

University Teaching & Research Affiliations Prior to Hofstra University

University of Arizona; University of New Hampshire; University of Massachusetts; Teachers College, Columbia University

New Undergraduate (UC), Masters (GC) & Doctoral (DC) Courses Developed (1998-2013)

Literacy, Art, Music and Dance (UC&GC); Family, Community, and School Literacies: Cultural Perspectives (GC); Literacy Learning at Home and in School: Social Contexts of Young Children Learning to Read and Write (GC); Children and Adolescents as Ethnographers in Communities and Schools (GC); Writing Pictures, Painting Stories as Mindful Social Practice (GC&DC); Family, Community, School and Workplace Literacy (GC&DC); Apprenticeship in the Ethnography of Literacy Research (DC); Advanced Seminar in the Ethnography of Literacy Research (DC); Works and Influence of Mikhail Bakhtin (DC); The Ethnographic Imagination: Existentialism, Empiricism, and the Philosophy of Mind (DC); Literacy Studies Sociolinguistics and Psycholinguistics Research Seminar (DC).

Honors

Invited Inaugural Fellow of the McKinnon Walker Trust, University of Wollongong, Australia, December, 2017

Elected Member of the International Reading Association's Reading Hall of Fame, May 2004.

Nominated for the Pulitzer Prize, 1997, for *Toxic Literacies: Exposing the Injustice of Bureaucratic Texts*.

Nominated for the National Book Award 1997, for Toxic Literacies: Exposing the Injustice of Bureaucratic Texts.

Ninth Annual Mina P. Shaughnessy Prize, Modern Language Association of America, 1989, for *Growing Up Literate: Learning From Inner City Families*.

CEE Richard A. Meade Award, National Council of Teachers of English, 1991, for Assessing the Complexity of Children's Literacy Learning, 1991.

International Reading Association's Outstanding Dissertation Award, finalist, 1981-82.

Philanthropic Gifts, Grants, & Awards

Philanthropic gift: from Richard Robinson, Scholastic Inc. for the publication of 500,000 copies of *The Kate Middleton Elementary School: Portraits of Hope and Courage* distributed to schools across the country in the aftermath of Hurricane Katrina, 2005;

Philanthropic gift: from the Angela and Scott Jaggar Foundation to support the International Scholar's Forums *Teachers Helping Teachers* and *Children Literacy and Trauma: Learning from Katrina's Teachers*, 2005 & 2007;

Philanthropic gift: from Jeffry Ordover for research on *Children and Mass Trauma*, administered by CELT 2008;

Southeastern Louisiana University Grant: in collaboration with Cindy Elliott [PI]: *Everybody's Child: Teacher Preparedness in Times of Crisis & Recovery*, 2007;

Elva Knight Research Award, International Reading Association, recipient, 1986-87; and co-recipient, 1982-83;

NCTE Research Foundation Award: *The City Literacy Project*, Laconia, New Hampshire, 1989-96. (This research was the basis of the book *Toxic Literacies: Exposing the Injustice of Bureaucratic Texts*, which was nominated by the publisher for the Pulitzer Prize.)

New Hampshire State Department of Education Grant: *The Biographic Literacy Profiles Project* (1988-94). Also sponsored by the Granite State Reading Association, and the Integrated Language Network. (This research was the basis of the book *From the Child's Point of View*.)

Founding Director of the International Center for Everybody's Child at Hofstra University

ICEC's Mission (2005-2013) to: (1) increase the social and psychological resources and educational opportunities provided to children who have experienced mass trauma; (2) strengthen their resiliency and recovery from trauma; and (3) engage children in activities created to enhance their emotional and physical well-being as well as their academic development and access to literacy. The work necessitated new ways of thinking about the interconnections between the social, psychological, biological, and physical sciences.

ICEC National Emergency activities include first response initiatives to Hurricanes Katrina, Rita & the Failure of the Levees First Response. International responses include initiatives undertaken in regions of armed conflict: Israel, the West Bank, and Gaza.

International presentations include: *Children and Mass Trauma* (American Consulate, Jerusalem, 2005; University of Bethlehem, 2005). Presentations in the U.S. include: *Earth's Children in Crisis: Inspiring the World to Action* (Hofstra University, 2009); *Darfur: What Can We Do?* (Hofstra University, 2007); *The World's Children in Crisis: What Can We Do?* (Hofstra University, 2007); *Children Literacy and Trauma: Learning from Katrina's Teachers*. (New York City, 2007)

Transdisciplinary Research in the Physical & Social Sciences & the Humanities

These on-going research endeavors in both the physical and social sciences focus on the complex interrelationships between: *Climate Change, Ecological Crisis, Global Economic Crisis, Armed Conflict, Public Health Emergencies, and Extreme Poverty*; *Empiricism, Existentialism and the Philosophy of Mind* (explorations in scientific and philosophical thought and our understandings of the world through language); *Social Cognition* (explorations of knowledge in practice in which time, space and setting are constitutive of the activity); *Semiotics, Aesthetics and Ethics* (explorations of the interface between functional texts and aesthetic scripts, illustration as visual essay, writing as an art form, lettering as design, the physicality of print, how tools and materials influence composition, and the production of texts as mindful social practice); *Historical Location of Emancipatory Systems of Meaning* (explorations resisting the dualities of the cognitive and the social; constructing explanations of the ways in which literacy is situated historically, politically, culturally, socially, linguistically, emotionally and biologically).

Founded, Organized, & Participated in Twenty-Two International Scholars Forums at Hofstra University (1998 -2008)

Mission: To participate in conversations with renowned scholars who have shaped our thinking, who are activists and advocates, and who struggle against racist and discriminatory practices.

Countries include: Australia; Brazil; Canada; Israel; Mexico; Rwanda; Sri Lanka; U.K.; & U.S.A.

Scholars include: JoBeth Allen (GA) 2005; Bess Altwerger (MD) 2002 & 2005; David Barton (U.K.) 1999 & 2003; Brian Cambourne (Australia) 1999 & 2008; Anne Haas Dyson (CA) 2007; Sarah Freedman (CA) 2005; Peter Fries (MI) 2007; James Gee (AZ) 2003; Kenneth Goodman (AZ) 1999; Yetta Goodman (Arizona) 1999 & 2001; Maxine Greene (NY) 2001; Kris Gutierrez (CA) 2004; Gunther Kress (U.K.) 2003; Prisca Martens (PA) 2008; Rick Meyer (NM) 2005; Sonia Nieto (MA) 2002; Kathy Short (AZ) 2003; Elvira Souza Lima (Brazil) 2001; Rick Meyer (NM)2005; Louise Rosenblatt (NJ) 2001; Nadeen Ruiz (CA) 1999; Margaret Meek Spencer (U.K.) 2001; Brian Street (U.K.) 2005; Lakshitha Saji Prelis (Sri Lanka) 2005; Frank Smith (Canada)2000; Steven S. Strauss (MD) 2002 & 2005; Brian Street (U.K.) 2003 & 2005; and Vivian Vasquez (DC) 2006.

Founded Garn Press to Support Writers of Conscience Providing Vital Information to the Public on the Perils Facing People and the Planet

Garn Press has three divisions: People and the Planet; People and Social Policy; Imagination and the Human Spirit.

Fiction books published:

You're Not Dead (2016, 2017 new edition), Geoff Ward, Principal of Homerton College and Deputy Vice-Chancellor, University of Cambridge, Chairman of the Fitzwilliam Museum Syndicate;

Blowing Out The Candles (2013, 2015), James Paul Gee, Mary Lou Fulton Presidential Professor at Arizona State University;

Black Inked Pearl: A Girl's Quest (2015), Ruth Finnegan, Emeritus Professor, The Open University, Fellow of the British Academy, Honorary Fellow of Somerville College Oxford;

Flush: The Exaggerated Memoir of a Fourth Grade Scaredy-Cat Super-Hero (2016), Rick Meyer, Professor and chair of the Department of Language, Literacy, & Sociocultural Studies, University of New Mexico;

Devil Knows (2015): A Tale of Murder and Madness in America's First Century (2015), David Joseph Kolb;

The Smart One (2015), Ken Goodman, Professor Emeritus, Language Reading and Culture, at the University of Arizona;

Bloody Lane (2015), Martin E. Lee, full-time freelance educational writer; and Matthew C. Fleury, freelance writer in English language arts educational publishing.

Non-fiction books:

The Educator And The Oligarch (2014, 2016), Anthony Cody, co-founder of the Network for Public Education, National Board certified teacher;

What's Whole in Whole Language in the 21st Century? (2014), Ken Goodman, Professor Emeritus, Language, Reading, and Culture, College of Education, University of Arizona;

Beware the Roadbuilders: Literature as Resistance (2015), P.L. Thomas, Professor of Education, Furman University, Greenville, SC;

Raising Peacemakers (2015), Esther Sokolov Fine, Professor Emerita of Education, York University, Toronto, Canada;

Preparing the Nation's Teachers to Teach Reading: A Manifesto in Defense of "Teacher Educators Like Me", (2015), Curt Dudley-Marling;

A Parent's Guide to Public Education in the 21st Century: Navigating Education Reform to Get the Best Education for My Child (2016), Russ Walsh, Public School Teacher and College Instructor;

5-13: A Memoir of Love, Loss and Survival (2016), Nancy Rankie Shelton, Professor of Education at UMBC in Baltimore, Maryland;

Negotiating a Permeable Curriculum: On Literacy, Diversity, and the Interplay of Children's and Teachers' Worlds (2016), Anne Haas Dyson, Faculty Excellence Professor, College of Education, University of Illinois at Urbana-Champaign; and Bobbie Kabuto, Associate Professor of Literacy Education in the Elementary and Early Childhood Education Department, Queens College, City University of New York;

First, Do No Harm: Progressive Education in a Time of Existential Risk (2016), Steve Nelson, Head of Calhoun School, NYC, 1998-2017;

Every Least Sparrow (2017), Carolyn H. Walker, journalist and creative writing instructor;

Trumplandia: Unmasking Post-Truth America (2017), P.L. Thomas, Professor of Education, Furman University, Greenville, SC;

United We Stand Divided We Fall: Resisting Trump's Agenda: Essays On Protest And Resistance And What We Can Do To Stop Him (2017); George Lakoff, Emeritus Professor of Cognitive Science and Linguistics at the University of California at Berkeley; Jonathan Foley, Executive Director of the California Academy of Sciences; Yohuru R. Williams, Professor and dean of the College of Arts and Sciences at the University of St. Thomas, Minnesota; and 14 other authors;

Playhouse: Optimistic Stories of Real Hope for Families with Little Children (2017), Monica Taylor, Professor and Deputy hair of the Department of Secondary and Special Education at Montclair State University;

The Gadfly on the Wall: A Public School Teacher Speaks Out on Racism and Reform (2017), Steven Singer, National Board Certified Language Arts teacher, Director of the Research and Blogging Committee for the Badass Teachers Association, and co-founder of the Pennsylvania-based education budget advocacy group T.E.A.C.H.

www.ingramcontent.com/pod-product-compliance
Lightning Source LLC
Chambersburg PA
CBHW041657040426
R18086800001B/R180868PG42333CBX00007B/5